Key Topics in Food
Science and Technology – No. 2

Waste management in the food industry
An overview

Gina Cybulska

Campden & Chorleywood Food Research Association Group comprises
Campden & Chorleywood Food Research Association
and its subsidiary companies
CCFRA Technology Ltd   CCFRA Group Services Ltd   Campden & Chorleywood Magyarország

Campden & Chorleywood Food
Research Association Group

Chipping Campden, Gloucestershire, GL55 6LD UK
Tel: +44 (0) 1386 842000   Fax: +44 (0) 1386 842100
www.campden.co.uk

© CCFRA 2000
ISBN: 0 905942 30 2

SERIES PREFACE

Food and food production have never had a higher profile, with food-related issues featuring in newspapers or on TV and radio almost every day. At the same time, educational opportunities related to food have never been greater. Food technology is taught in schools, as a subject in its own right, and there is a variety of food-related courses in colleges and universities - from food science and technology (FST) through nutrition and dietetics to catering and hospitality management.

Despite this attention, there is widespread misunderstanding of food - about what it is, about where it comes from, about how it is produced, and about its role in our lives. One reason for this, perhaps, is that the consumer has become distanced from the food production system as it has become much more sophisticated in response to the developing market for choice and convenience. Whilst other initiatives are addressing the issue of consumer awareness, feedback from the food industry itself and from the educational sector has highlighted the need for short focused overviews of specific aspects of food science and technology with an emphasis on industrial relevance.

The *Key Topics in Food Science and Technology* series of short books therefore sets out to describe some fundamentals of food and food production, and in addressing a specific topic, each issue emphasises the principles and illustrates their application through industrial examples. Although aimed primarily at food industry recruits and trainees, the series will also be of interest to those interested in a career in the food industry, FST students, food technology teachers, trainee enforcement officers and, established personnel within industry seeking a broad overview of particular topics.

Leighton Jones
Series Editor

PREFACE TO THIS VOLUME

Waste is a global issue that affects us all. It has a potentially deleterious effect on the environment and human health and there are major initiatives, on an international level, to address its production and management. These initiatives continue to bring about changes in attitude which are impinging on our lives daily, through, for example, new legislation and controls to encourage the choice of more environmentally friendly options for the management and disposal of waste.

These developments are as important to the food and allied industries as to any other sector. The food industry, like other sectors, consumes both renewable and non-renewable materials and is constantly seeking improved efficiency of energy and material utilisation. It faces a changing legislative framework in which to operate and sells its products to consumers who too are increasingly aware of 'environmental issues'.

This book sets out to provide a general overview of waste and waste management, as it relates to the activities of the food production and supply chain. It discusses what waste is, how it is generated and how the options for waste can be assessed in terms of the 'waste management hierarchy'. It gives examples of how the food industry can participate in the re-use and recycling of materials, and provides an introduction to the concepts and potential benefits of 'environmental quality management' and 'life cycle analysis'. It also provides an overview of legislation and related controls impinging on waste in the EU and UK. It is emphasised that it is not intended as a detailed reference guide on waste legislation, but to illustrate main concepts and current thinking.

Gina Cybulska
CCFRA, May 2000

ACKNOWLEDGEMENTS

I would like to express my sincere thanks to Chris Knight, David Dawson, John Hammond, Leighton Jones, Tim Hutton and Celia Willcox (CCFRA) and Heather Cholerton (Waste Management Information Bureau) for their comments and advice. Thanks are also due to Janette Stewart for the artwork and design.

NOTE

All definitions, legislation, codes of practice, disposal mechanisms and guidelines in this publication are included for the purposes of illustration and relate to UK practice unless otherwise stated.

CONTENTS

1. WASTE

The production and management of waste is a global issue that affects us all. Increasing concerns about the environmental impact of waste and its potential effects on health have led to the establishment of stringent legislation in many countries, which has affected and will continue to affect industry and householders.

1.1 What is waste?

Waste is generally thought of as something that is no longer needed by the original user and is subsequently discarded. It is defined in UK legislation as "any substance which constitutes a scrap material or an effluent or other unwanted surplus substance arising from the application of any process"[1]. It is further defined as "any substance or article which requires to be disposed of as being broken, worn out, contaminated or otherwise spoiled"[1], or that "the holder discards, intends to or is required to discard"[2] (based on the definition of waste in EC Directive 91/156/EEC)[121, 155].

To define something as a waste, it should be or will be discarded by its producer[121]. But when something constitutes a waste is by no means clear, especially with regards to whether something is a waste, co-product, or a by-product, or a "raw" material for reprocessing (i.e. recycling operations). For this reason, details as to how to determine whether an item constitutes "waste" are discussed in the Department of the Environment Circular 11/94 on the Waste Management Licensing Regulations[121,156,157], though it is also covered by other regulations. Ultimately, however, the definition is subject to interpretation in courts of law. Recently, for example, in the 1998 case *Mayer Parry Recycling Ltd v Environment Agency*[30, 152], there was extensive debate as to whether scrap metal, subjected to a recycling operation, constituted a waste[152]. For the purpose of this review, therefore, waste will simply be regarded as material that is not wanted by its producer.

Waste comes from just about all processes or systems. It is generated by all companies and from any type of organisation or institution and by individuals. If the waste comes from household, industrial or commercial sources it is defined as a controlled waste[1] (Table 1) and requires specific measures for its treatment and disposal[3]. This means that it must follow the waste management licensing regime and comply with the Duty of Care and the requirement for waste carriers to be registered[4,145,158] (see Chapter 6 for further information on controls).

Table 1 - Sources of Waste Classified as Controlled Waste[1,3]

Category	Sources
Household waste	Domestic property Caravans Residential homes Premises forming part of educational establishments Premises forming part of a hospital or nursing home
Industrial waste	Any factory Any premises that are connected with or provide public transport by means of land, air or water Any premises that are connected with or supply the public with gas, water, electricity or sewerage services Any premises used for the purposes of postal or telecommunications services
Commercial waste	Waste from a premises used wholly or mainly for the trade or business or the purposes of sport, recreation or entertaining excluding: ● Household waste ● Industrial waste ● Waste from a mine or quarry ● Waste from premises used for agriculture

Agricultural waste, i.e. all waste from premises used for agriculture (as originally defined in the Agricultural Act 1947), is not classified as controlled waste[4]. This means that no waste management licence is required for the disposal of agricultural waste and so it may be disposed of at the site that generated the waste, as long as some pollution prevention measures are taken. Proposals have been put forward to classify some agricultural wastes as controlled wastes, but these measures have yet to be implemented.

1.2 Management and control of waste

The measures used to manage waste are driven by legislation, which specifies what constitutes waste and encourages particular treatment or disposal options. This is done through, for example, attaching financial penalties to the less preferred options (e.g. the landfill tax) or by setting recycling targets for a particular waste type (e.g. packaging waste) or targets for a particular disposal method (e.g. reducing the volume of waste disposed to landfill). UK legislation on the control of waste began in earnest in the 1970s (although earlier controls existed), after sodium cyanide waste was dumped in a children's play area in Coventry[83, 121]. Moves to harmonisation within the European Union means that most current control measures are based on EU legislation which member states will have been required to integrate into their national law.

The UK implements EU legislation through setting Acts of Parliament, which are then further defined through Statutory Instruments. For example the EC Directive 94/62/EC on packaging waste is incorporated into UK law via the Environment Act 1995 in the section on producer responsibility (Sections 93-95)[2]. Here the provision is set up to increase the "re-use, recovery or recycling of products or materials"[2]. This could apply to any product or material, although the only one that currently comes under this provision is packaging waste. The details of the packaging waste scheme are set out in the Producer Responsibility Obligations (Packaging Waste) Regulations 1997, Statutory Instrument 1997 No. 648 (as amended).

The legislation mentioned in this review relates to the original items that came into force, but it should be remembered that this is subject to on-going amendment. The intention here is not to provide detailed guidance on the legislation but to illustrate the broad ideas behind the core legislation and how these influence trends and developments in waste management.

In the wake of legislative pressure to bring about changes in waste production and disposal, a number of quality management systems have been established to help companies to monitor their environmental impact and manage their activities. The uptake of these are low within the food industry, in comparison to, for example, the chemical industry. Most of these initiatives, through legislation and quality management, place some sort of reliance on data, which requires an informed understanding of, for example, quantities of waste generated, energy consumed and the volume of water used. While it is evident that there is currently a distinct lack of hard facts and statistics with regards to volumes of waste produced, Government and industry now recognise this and measures are being implemented to assess waste output to provide useful benchmarks for future waste management strategies.

1.3 Waste management in the food industry

With waste production and disposal under increasing scrutiny and with companies facing increasing legislative and economic incentives to manage waste efficiently, this review sets out to provide a broad overview of the issues, particularly as they relate to the food and allied industries. By following the food production chain it describes how waste is generated, how it is treated (e.g. reused, recycled, or disposed of) and then looks at how the management of waste is regulated. It also provides pointers to sources of much more detailed information on many of the complex issues that can arise with regard to waste management and can act as a starting point for taking further action.

2. WASTE SOURCES AND DISPOSAL PRACTICES

A wide range of wastes is produced by various sub-sectors of the food and drink industry. This review gives an overview of the types of waste that can occur. The main disposal methods of these wastes are given, but other methods may be viable.

There is a lack of information available on the volumes of food industry waste produced and the current disposal routes for the waste generated. The Environment Agency has recently undertaken a study to determine the volume of industrial and commercial wastes generated by all industries and the results should be made available in a national database in the near future. Initial results from this study indicate that the food, drink and tobacco sector contributes 8-11 million tonnes per annum to the industrial/commercial total of 70-100 million tonnes/year[5] (Figure 1). This partly reflects the importance and size of the food and drink industry within the UK.

Figure 1 - The percentage of total industrial and commercial waste generated by the food industry

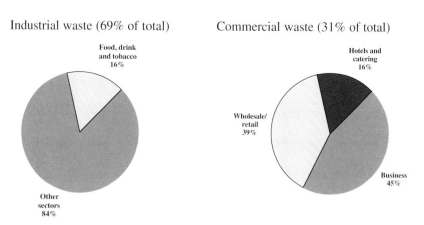

Industrial waste (69% of total)

Commercial waste (31% of total)

Waste generated by the food, drink and tobacco sector accounts for around 16% of industrial waste, which itself makes up 69% of combined industrial and commercial waste. Wholesale (including food and drink) accounts for 39% and hotels and catering for 16% of commercial waste, which itself makes up 31% of the combined industrial and commercial waste.

To get food from the field to the plate involves a sophisticated production and supply chain, but for the purposes of waste production this can be simplified to three main steps: agriculture, food processors/manufacturers and the retail/commercial sector. Each of the sectors generates waste and some wastes are common to all sectors, such as packaging waste and washwater; other wastes may be specific to two of the sectors (e.g. manure from agriculture and manure from abattoirs). Some wastes are highly specific to the particular sector of the industry, e.g. washwater from lye peeling of vegetables. Figure 2 summaries the main wastes generated from each stage of the food chain.

Figure 2 - Examples of waste from the different stages in the food production chain

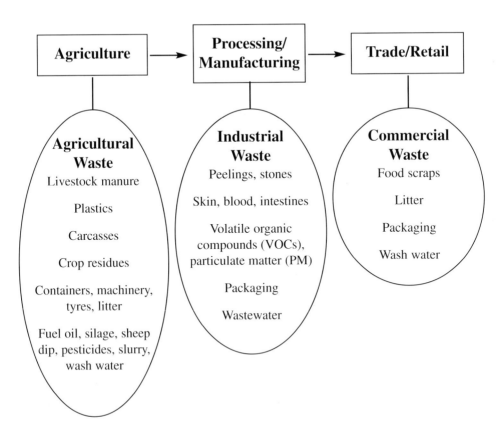

The following sections cover some of the solid, liquid and gaseous wastes produced in each of these three stages of the food production chain and their disposal routes. More detailed information on the disposal options, e.g. anaerobic digestion, incineration, composting and landfilling, is presented in Chapter 3.

2.1 Agricultural waste

Some agricultural waste can be very polluting and farmers are required to take measures to control the storage and disposal of the waste in an environmentally sound manner[1]. Guidelines have been published by government departments on the collection, storage and disposal of agricultural waste. These provide information on the design and siting of storage facilities, and the collection and storage of waste from animal housing, livestock yards, feed preparation areas, dairies, slurry pits and operational management[7].

The enforcement agencies are promoting the use of farm waste management plans in order to help farmers manage the organic waste generated on their establishments as well as any waste received for the purpose of landspreading (see Chapter 4). The plans identify methods of collection and storage and give guidance on the application of waste to the land[8].

Agricultural wastes are not controlled wastes under the definition in the Environmental Protection Act 1990[1] and so no waste management licence is required to dispose of the waste. Farmers can therefore dispose of the waste on their own land by burying, spreading or burning the waste.

Burying of waste material is allowed as long as certain measures are taken[9]. These measures include:

◆   Maintaining a specified minimum distance from watercourses.
◆   Recording details of burial sites.
◆   Ensuring sufficient burial depth.

Features that have to be considered when spreading waste on land include[10]:

◆ The rate of application.
◆ The slope of the ground.
◆ The condition of the soil (waterlogged, frozen or covered in snow prohibits landspreading).
◆ Appropriate distance from watercourses.
◆ Minimising the effect on neighbours, such as noise and odours.

Burning of waste is allowed unless:

◆ There is production of dark smoke[11], which is defined as finely divided particles of matter suspended in air as a visible cloud[12].
◆ Other reasonably safe and practicable methods of disposing of the waste are available[12].

Where the burning is completed in an incinerator that operates at a rate of more than 50kg/hr, approval for the incinerator must be granted by the local authority[12].

Waste minimisation also plays a part in controlling agricultural wastes. Research has been undertaken by the Government and the Environment Agency into agricultural waste minimisation, and will subsequently result in a guide[13, 14].

Under the EC Directive on Waste (75/442/EEC as amended by 91/156/EEC), there will be a move to classify some agricultural waste (non-organic and household)[83] as controlled[4], although the timescale for this is not apparent. This means that the methods of disposal of these wastes will change when these regulations are brought in. The information on agricultural wastes in the following sections is a very brief overview of the current situation, as stated in the various Codes of Good Agricultural Practice available from MAFF and SOAFED[7, 12, 15, 16, 17].

2.1.1 Solid Waste

Solid agricultural waste includes by-products resulting from livestock and crop management and equipment used for managing the farm.

Manure

The management of manure plays an important part in the management of agricultural wastes due to the sheer volume produced. Recent studies indicate that 80 million tonnes of by-products from housed livestock needs to be dealt with per year[27].

Table 2 - Amount of excreta produced from farm animals[7]

Type of livestock	Typical volume (litres/day)
1 dairy cow	35-57
1 lactating sow and litter	15
1 mature sheep	4
1000 laying hens	115

Example - Pig slurry

On one farm in Australia, piggery waste was treated by anaerobic digestion. An average of 210,000 litres of slurry was produced on a daily basis on one farm, and 50 tonnes of manure was spread on land per week. The digestion system has resulted in the production of an odourless organic fertiliser, while the biogas is used to generate electricity and heat.

Reference:

Anaerobic digestion of piggery wastes in Victoria, Australia", CADDET Technical Brochure No. 4. (Reference 28).

Example - Poultry litter

Poultry litter has a gross calorific value of 13.5GJ per tonne. A power station was constructed in the UK and poultry litter from 50 poultry-rearing businesses from the vicinity of the power station was burnt. The plant generated 12.7 MW of electricity per year, enough to power 13,000 homes, using 130,000 tonnes of litter annually.

Reference:

"Poultry litter power station in the United Kingdom", CADDET Technical Brochure No. 17. (Reference 29).

Manure can be disposed of in the following ways:

- ♦ Aerobic and anaerobic digestion - the volume and odour of manure is significantly reduced and the resulting mass can be used on the land.
- ♦ Spread on land - without any pre-treatment. The high nutrient content of manure can be recycled back into the land, thereby reducing the level of manufactured fertilisers being applied.
- ♦ Incinerated - poultry litter has been used as a fuel source.

Farm Plastics/Films

Plastic film is used in agriculture for a number of purposes, including covering for baled hay and silage heaps. Other plastic wastes generated on farms include polythene from fertiliser bags, pallet covers and covers from crop production greenhouses[7]. In 1996, 77,386 tonnes of farm plastic film waste was generated in England and Wales[27].

Farmers have tended to dispose of their plastic waste by burial or burning. However, this may change if some agricultural waste is classified as a controlled waste and will effectively halt disposal of these wastes on the farm[27]. A voluntary collection and recycling scheme for farm plastics was once in place, but the scheme collapsed in 1997. A consultation paper was issued by the DETR in 1998 "Options for tackling the problem of waste non-packaging farm plastics". The options proposed were to set up another voluntary scheme or to introduce Producer Responsibility regulations, which place statutory obligations on the manufacturers to recover farm plastics[27]. While the first option is favoured, no scheme in England has yet to be established.

Animal carcasses

Animal carcasses result from the normal death of the animal, or death through disease. In some instances, appropriate authorities need to be notified of the death of an animal from a particular disease and the only effective method of disposal of these diseased carcasses is by incineration[7].

The main methods of disposal of carcasses are by a licensed knackerman, hunt kennel, licensed landfill operator or incinerator. Where these options are not viable, carcasses can be disposed of on the farm[7].

Disposal on the farm can be by burial or burning, either in an incinerator, or in the open:

●   Burial of carcasses

Where there is no instance of a notifiable disease, the carcass can be buried so long as it does not pollute the environment. Burial sites must be sufficiently covered to prevent access from scavenging animals and birds and detailed plans of burial sites must be maintained[9].

●   Incineration of carcasses

Carcasses can be destroyed in an incinerator. Specific temperatures need to be maintained to ensure efficient and complete destruction of the carcasses in order to prevent the spread of disease through the atmosphere. This means that compliance with Integrated Pollution Control (IPC) guidance is necessary (see Chapter 6). Carcasses can also be incinerated in the open air, but precautions must be taken to prevent the fire from spreading and to minimise public exposure[9].

Example - Cattle and BSE

In 1996, under the Florence Framework, the UK Government undertook measures to selectively slaughter animals considered to be at a high risk of developing BSE, in order to accelerate the eradication of BSE[31]. Under these measures, carcasses have to be rendered and destroyed or destroyed directly. The following table shows the number of cattle that have been slaughtered.

Table 3 - Number of cattle slaughtered as part of the BSE eradication. Numbers shown up to the end of October 1999[31].

Regions	Abattoirs	Incinerators	Total
England	2,022,360	174,687	2,197,047
Wales	334,809	57,169	391,978
Scotland	485,123	18,967	504,090
N Ireland	525,308	0	525,308
UK	3,367,600	250,823	3,618,423

Plant and plant products

Plant product wastes include crop residues such as straw stubble, residues of oilseed rape, field beans and dry harvested peas, wood waste from pruning in orchards and wood used in the maintenance of buildings[12]. Other types of plant waste include trimmings, peelings, plant debris and soil residues from the processing that takes place on the farm[17].

The burning of materials such as straw stubble is banned in England and Wales under the Crop Residues (Burning) Regulations 1993[32], unless there are extenuating circumstances (e.g.: disease control)[12]. Burning is permitted in Scotland, but even without prohibition by law, less than 5% of Scottish stubbles are currently burnt[7].

The problem with the disposal of plant residues is to ensure that no pests or diseases, such as potato brown rot or Colorado beetles, are spread[17]. Under specific conditions, Parliament has powers to enact legislation to enforce particular disposal methods to limit the spread of any pests or disease.

Other methods of management for plant crop waste include:

Reduction of waste:

◆ Cleaning the root crops in the fields to reduce soil adhesion[17].
◆ Trimming and grading in the field. The excesses can be left to be grazed by livestock or ploughed back into the field[17].

Reuse of waste:

◆ Any solid waste, such as straw and crop residues, could be used as a growing medium, mulch, soil improver, fertiliser or animal feed[17].
◆ Straw could also be used as a pulp for paper and board production (although outlets/markets need to be arranged) or used as a fuel[17].
◆ Sugar beet pulp, which is an absorbent material, could be used to soak up silage effluent[7].

The final disposal option is to a licensed landfill or incinerator, or to a composting plant. In some instances it may be necessary to dispose of some plant waste to an incinerator in order to ensure that diseases are not spread, or to ensure that the crop is not capable of regrowth[17].

Containers, tyres, machinery, litter

There are a number of wastes not specific to agriculture, but which are nevertheless generated by the agricultural sector and still require some form of disposal. Examples include tyres, plastics, scrap machinery and household waste[7, 9]. As these items are classed as agricultural waste (see Chapter 1), there is no restriction on their disposal, but the enforcement agencies encourage waste minimisation and the recycling of these items.

These materials can be recycled on the farm (e.g. through using tyres to retain plastic sheeting on silage pits) or sent to dedicated recycling facilities that are available. The waste can also be disposed of at licensed waste management facilities by using waste management contractors[7]. This is the preferred method of disposal for pesticide containers.

2.1.2 Liquid wastes

Agricultural fuel oil and waste oils

This type of waste is generated through the maintenance and use of machinery and includes lubricating oils and fuel oils. As oil is highly polluting, special measures are required to minimise any potential pollution such as appropriate design of storage facilities, construction, location, operation and maintenance[7].

Some waste oil can be reused as a fuel for heaters, but the main method for disposal is at a licensed waste management facility[62].

Silage effluent

Silage effluent is liquid produced during the storage of silage. It is highly polluting and can corrode steel and concrete. Specific measures are required for storage of the effluent to minimise any pollution risk[7]. Two main methods for disposal include:

- Land application, as it contains high levels of nutrients including nitrogen, phosphates, magnesium and potassium which are recycled back into the land[7].
- Feeding it to livestock after treatment[63].

Sheep dip

Sheep dip wastes result from any product that is not used and the remnants of dip after being used[7, 64]. The possible disposal options include:

- Treatment on advice from the manufacturer.
- Returning concentrated dip to the manufacturers.

- ◆ Disposal by a licensed waste management contractor.
- ◆ Crushing empty containers and disposal of by a licensed waste management contractor (thereby preventing reuse of the containers).
- ◆ Disposal to land (this is not a common method of disposal)[7, 64].

Disposal of sheep dip and pesticides is controlled by the Groundwater Regulations[119], which aim to minimise the pollution of underground stores of water.

Pesticides

Pesticides can be highly polluting, but effective handling and usage can minimise the amount of waste generated[65]. With the wider adoption of integrated crop management systems, this is now happening[66]. There is also a growing awareness of the use of Hazard Analysis Critical Control Point (HACCP) approaches as part of pesticide use strategies[67]. A HACCP approach can provide an effective and cost-effective, logical and structured means of providing a pesticide control system[67].

Possible disposal options for pesticide related waste include[65]:

- ◆ Packaging - returned to suppliers or disposed of by waste management contractors. The British Agrochemicals Association has developed guidelines on the disposal of pesticides and pesticide containers and has developed a cheap and effective small-scale incinerator for on-farm burning[153].
- ◆ Concentrates - returned to manufacturer or disposed of by waste management contractors.
- ◆ Dilute wastes - are either sprayed following specific guidelines or disposed of by a waste management contractor.

Slurry

Slurry is a mixture of animal manure and bedding, feed residues, rainwater and wash water[10]. It contains approximately 3% to 12% solid matter[16]. It also contains high levels of nutrients and recycling them back to the land can reduce the level of manufactured fertilisers applied to the land[10]. However, slurry is highly polluting and can promote weed and algae growth which strip oxygen from water, killing aquatic life[10].

Slurry can be applied to land, but there are restrictions on the rate of application and the concentration of the slurry. Alternatively, it can be treated aerobically (to reduce its volume and allowing it to be stored for later use) or dilute slurry can be passed through reed beds, where the roots of the reeds reduce the biological oxygen demand of the material[7]. Slurry, manure and sewage sludge can contain pathogenic bacteria. There is some interest in the safe use of manures and slurry - focusing on composting and extended storage times to reduce the levels of bacteria, but no guidelines are yet available.

Washwater

This is produced from the cleaning of crops, buildings and yards[17]. Washwater can be recirculated after treatment, to remove suspended solids. Treatment methods include ultraviolet irradiation, heat treatment, microfiltration, ozonation and disinfection by non-persistent chemicals such as peracetic acid[17]. Otherwise, treated washwater can be disposed of to watercourses and/or sewers as long as discharge consent has been obtained from the appropriate authorities[17].

2.1.3 Gaseous waste

There are two main gaseous waste categories from agricultural establishments: odours and ammonia. Particulate matter from grain harvesting could also be classed as an emission to air[73].

Odours

Odours from farm premises are a major cause of complaint. In 1995/96, over 9,000 complaints were received in England and Wales involving 3,646 farm premises. The establishments which caused the greatest number of complaints were from pig farms, followed by poultry. The main process that raised odour complaints was the application of slurry and manure to land[12]. Sources of odours stem mainly from the breakdown of slurries, silage effluent and solid manure. Other sources include waste food, animal scents and animal feed[12].

The degree of odour resulting from spreading slurry on land is dependent on the source of the waste (pigs, cattle, poultry), whether there are other wastes included in the slurry (milk or silage effluent) and the method by which the slurry is spread on the land[12].

Gaseous emissions can be controlled by:

- Treating the slurry by aerobic or anaerobic digestion, which reduces the odour and allows storage of the resulting mass[12].
- Treating emission from buildings by air cleaning systems[12].
- Treating the emissions by using oxidising agents, deodorants, masking and biological agents, feed additives and electrolytic methods, which tend to be used as temporary measures[12].
- Farmers monitoring weather conditions and choosing the appropriate spreading methods to minimise the odour[12].

Ammonia

Ammonia results from the breakdown of urea in animal manures, on contact with air, and agriculture is one of the main producers of ammonia emissions. Of the total ammonia emissions from farmland, 40% is directly from livestock and 30% is from spreading slurry on land. The remaining fractions come from manure storage, fertilisers and grazing livestock[12]. Ways of minimising ammonia emissions include:

- Restricting the amount of protein in the animal diet. Up to 60-80% of nitrogen in feed is excreted[12].
- Effective management of livestock housing and slurry/manure stores. This is done through effective cleaning and limiting exposure of the slurry to air[12].

Particulate matter (PM)

This occurs in the harvesting of grain, from handling the crop, loading it onto transport and transporting it[73].

Greenhouse heaters

These are used to maintain a constant temperature. The main emissions are from the fuel and include carbon dioxide[73]. The flue gases are recycled back into the glass-houses, where the increased levels of CO_2 boost crop yields.

Pesticide application

The main emissions are organic compounds and particulate matter. The active ingredients in pesticides tend to be slightly volatile and may also contain volatile solvents (e.g. xylene) and emulsifiers[73].

2.2 Food processing waste

Wastes from food processing are recycled back into the food processing chain as well as being disposed of via landfill. Measures to minimise waste are beginning to play an important role in the reduction of disposal costs and volumes. It has been suggested that companies incur costs of over £50,000 in disposal of solid and liquid wastes for every £1 million spent on ingredients[18].

The type of processing waste generated depends on the food that is being processed (Table 4), but the main type of waste produced by all sectors of the food processing industry is wastewater. This results from the cleaning of the raw materials, treatment/cooking of the food and cleaning of the equipment. A substantial amount of information on the treatment of wastewater from different areas of the food processing industry is available and is covered in journals such as Bioresource Technology[19], Water Environment Research[20] and Water Science and Technology[21], amongst others. Though there is less information on the solid wastes produced, it is evident that a large amount of solid food processing waste is recycled, either to produce animal feeds, or after further processing to produce products that are used for non-food purposes.

Table 4 - Amounts of waste generated from processing of food[22]

Processed food waste	Total solid (g/kg)	Liquid volume (m³/kg)
Vegetables		
Kale	16	0.004
Spinach	20	
Mustard greens	16	
Turnip greens	15	
Potatoes	66	0.012
Peppers (caustic peeling)	65	0.020
Tomatoes (caustic peeling)	14	0.010
Dairy		
Cheese whey		9.00
Skim milk		0.07
Ice cream		0.08
Meat		
Red	0.44	25.00
Poultry	0.27	50.00
Eggs	0.111	

While information is available on technologies to treat the waste (especially wastewater), there are no statistics available for the actual volume of waste produced. This is probably because each individual plant produces different quantities and qualities of waste[23]. Variations in the waste stream can be caused by seasonal differences, type of product, processing methods, method of picking the crop and activities of the plant at the time of sampling[23]. It would not be reliable, therefore, to extrapolate the data gathered from one plant to the whole of the industry, with any degree of accuracy.

The disposal and treatment of wastewater is controlled by various trade effluent regulations. These specify restrictions on disposal of wastewater to sewers and watercourses, such as the levels of certain chemicals and the requirement to inform the enforcement agencies and the sewerage undertakers of any discharges. Discharge consents are required, which detail the amount of effluent, rate of discharge, temperature, pH and the limits for polluting matter. Regular monitoring is required to ensure that the discharged effluent remains within the limits set by the consent[24].

The treatment of any effluent is dependent on its strength. This has a resulting impact on the storage, treatment and disposal method of the wastewater, and subsequently, the cost of the overall process. The two main categories for defining the strength of the wastewater are:

- Biological Oxygen Demand (BOD)
  This is a measure of the biodegradable material in the effluent and is determined by measuring the quantity of oxygen consumed when stored at 20°C for five days[25, 151].
- Chemical Oxygen Demand (COD)
  This is a measure of oxygen required for the oxidation of all organic matter in the effluent, using chemical oxidants such as dichromate[25, 151].

Other parameters that define the strength and subsequent treatment options include the volume produced, suspended solids, total solids, grease, fat and oil content, nitrogen concentration, pathogenic microorganisms, temperature and colour[25].

As each plant and process produces different quantities and qualities of wastewater, it is necessary to monitor each site individually to ensure proper treatment of the effluent produced at that plant[26].

2.2.1 Solid wastes

It is difficult to determine the amount of solid wastes generated by food processing and the methods by which they are disposed of, as most of the literature on the food processing industry concentrates on the treatment of liquid effluents. From the literature that is available it is evident that the solid waste is either used as animal feed[83], spread on land for use as a fertiliser or disposed of to waste management facilities. Table 5 summarises some of the typical wastes generated from a selection of food processing areas and some routes for reuse and disposal.

The treatment of wastewater results in the production of sludges, which are treated as a solid waste. Other solid wastes include containers for the raw materials, packaging and broken bottles[37].

Table 5 - Examples of waste produced in food processing and traditional disposal routes

Processing Facility	Typical Solid Wastes	Disposal Option
Meat processing	Dependent on the type of animal, includes: Hide/skin, bone, intestines, feathers, hair, fats; parts not used (head, feet, intestines)[33, 34].	• Hides - leather industry[33]. • Blood - production of protein powders, or plasma used as an egg white substitute, cloth printing, emulsifiers, liquid clarifier in sugar and wine processing[33]. • Haemoglobin - glue, meal[33]. • Bones - gelatin and bone meal[33]. • Offal - fertiliser[33]. • Stomach contents - landfilled[33]. • Stomach lining - sausage skins, surgical sutures and tennis racquets[34]. • Fats, grease and fine particulates - animal feed, soap, synthetics e.g. tyres, lubricants and cosmetics[25]; also margarine, cooking fats[34].
Seafood processing	Whole fish, skin, shells (in crab processing, up to 85% is waste[23].)	• Whole fish, protein material - fish meal[23]. • Composted/landfilled.
Fruit and vegetable	Peelings, stones, leaves, spices waste[35].	• Composted/landfilled. • Animal feed
Bakery	Waste bread, flour, masa, yeast[35].	• Landfill. • Animal feed
Sugar	Molasses, bagasse[36].	• Composted/landfill. • Fuel • Feed for yeast production[35]. • Animal feed
Dairy	Containers Dried milk, butter, buttermilk residues, cheese, whey, suspended solids[35].	• Landfill • Animal feed

Table 6: Examples of food processing waste and how it can be used

Food waste	Use
Animal fat	Biosurfactant production[38]
Orange peel	Dietary fibre[39]
Lemon peel	Source of flavanoids[40]
Molasses Grape skin pulp extract Starch waste Potato pulp Olive oil effluent	Production of ethanol[41, 42]
Breadcrumbs	Production of sourdough[43]
Brewery grain	Compost for mushrooms Used to cultivate earthworms for chicken feed[44]
Fish waste	Protein hydrolysates[45]
Onion wastes	Onion oil, fructooligosaccharides, pectic polysaccharides and low-lignin dietary fibre[46]
Stones from peaches, nectarines, plums, apricots, olives and cherries	Charcoal[37]
Bagasse	Fuel Sold to pulp and paper industry[47]
Rice husk	Cementious material Fuel[48]
Nut shells	Activated carbon (to absorb chemicals such as metal-based pollutants from water)[49]
Coffee husks	Fuel[50]
Palm oil shell	Aggregate in lightweight concrete[51]

Example - Potato peeling sludge

Lye peeling of potatoes (i.e. using sodium hydroxide to promote the peeling) produces a sludge that can be recycled, and increases the amount of product obtained, reducing the amount of solid waste. But the resulting wastewater has a high pH, and requires treatment before disposal. Although the wastewater resulting from steam peeling does not have this problem[37], up to four times more water is used by this process than the dry caustic peeling process[23].

As the volume of food processing wastes is high, research is constantly being undertaken to determine alternative disposal routes. Table 6 summarises some of the alternative uses already found.

In order to minimise waste, changes to the production line may be needed. Any improvements should decrease the volume of waste produced and increase the production line efficiency. Changes to the process may result in different wastes being produced and it is therefore necessary to ensure that all costs and wastes are taken into account[23, 37].

Recovery of solid wastes from liquid effluent is needed in order to treat the effluent more efficiently and to ensure that all the by-products of the process are recovered for reuse. Some of the procedures used to separate the solid waste from the liquid effluent include:

- Ion exchange to recover amino acids, potassium, organic acids, phosphates and proteins.
- Ultrafiltration to recover large molecular proteins such as whey proteins.
- Flocculation/precipitation to recover large molecular proteins from meat processing.
- Reverse osmosis to recover citrus products. .
- Spray drying of solutions to produce a powder to be reused (e.g. blood protein powder).
- Brine fermentation to reduce the salt content. This reduces the amount of sodium chloride disposed to sewer and the resulting salt can be used in, for example, olive mills to store freshly harvested crop before processing[37].

Other solid wastes that are produced include the containers which stored the incoming raw materials. Companies that supply the raw materials may operate a take-back service or the processing company may send the various containers for recycling[37].

2.2.2 Liquid wastes

Wastewater from the processing industry is the main waste stream that is produced. Wastewater results from using water as a coolant and from washing, trimming, blanching and pasteurising[23]. The effluent may contain colour (e.g. from beet processing), soil, lye, insecticides and solids[23]. Also a large amount of water is used for cleaning equipment (see Table 7).

Table 7 - The percentage of total water used for cleaning[68]

Type of site	Cleaning water use (%)
Bakery	70
Soft drinks manufacturer	48
Brewery	45
Jam manufacturer	22

Most food and drinks companies discharge effluent to sewer and have to pay a discharge levy related to the strength and the volume of the effluent. Table 8 shows how the cost of treating effluent relates to the COD value of the effluent.

Table 8 - Typical COD values and costs of the effluent treatment (1998)[68]

Product	Typical COD value mg/kg product	Typical effluent cost pence/kg product
Sugar	1,000,000	36
Cream	700,000	25
Yeast	400,000	14
Starch	200,000	7
Blood	200,000	7
Beer	200,000	7
Milk	160,000	6
Orange juice	80,000 (BOD)	3

The actual volumes of liquid wastes produced are very difficult to determine as there is little published on the quantity and quality of effluent output from individual plants. The contents of effluents vary with the particular processing operation:

◆   Meat processing: Typical effluents contain blood, fats, organic and inorganic solids, salts and chemicals added during processing[23].

◆   Seafood processing: Water from cutting, washing and processing, which may contain blood, skins, viscera, condensate from the cooking operation and cooking water[23].

◆   Fruit and vegetable processing: Effluent contents include carbohydrates, pectins, vitamins and components of cell walls. Up to 70-85% organic matter is present in the effluent in dissolved form[23].

◆   Dairy processing: Most of the waste from dairy processing is effluent, containing whole and processed milk, and whey from cheese production, which means a high amount of dissolved organic compounds. It may also contain cleaning effluent[23].

There are two main options for the treatment of wastewater - on-site or by the water companies or authorities. The available options depend largely on factors like the size of the operation, location, volumes produced, available treatment works and available watercourses. Examples of technologies for treating wastewater are in Table 9.

On-Site Treatment

This option usually takes place where it has historically been done or is cheaper. It is also used when the effluent cannot be passed to the water company or authority for treatment, or the discharge consents set by the water authorities and enforcement agencies cannot be met[26]. The effluent can be treated in three stages:

◆   Primary Treatment - physical separation of solid matter to prevent blockages in pipes and within the treatment plant and reduce the COD load. Techniques include screening by various methods including stationary screens, rotary cylindrical screens, brushed screens and vibrating screens, coarse filtration, fat traps and settlement. Other treatment methods include dissolved air flotation, and ion exchange, reverse osmosis and ultrafiltration[25].

Table 9: Technologies available for physically treating dissolved substances and suspended solids in effluent[70]

Technology	Process
Adsorption	Physical or chemical process where the substance becomes bound to a surface (e.g. activated carbon) and is removed from the liquid stream.
Ion exchange	This depends on the interchange of ions between a solution and the surface of the ion exchange material.
Precipitation	The addition of a chemical agent to cause a dissolved substance to precipitate out
Membrane technologies	These allow specific substances to pass through the membrane, but retain others; includes reverse osmosis, which prevents low molecular weight molecules from passing through; and ultrafiltration which will retain large molecular weight molecules
Electrical technologies	The use of an electrical current to change a feed system, e.g. removal of metal ions
Evaporation	The use of heat and sometimes pressure to vaporise and remove one of more components from the stream
Distillation	This exploits the different volatilities of the components
Dissolved air flotation	Physical separation by micro-bubbles of air, which become attached to the suspended matter. Sometimes chemical additives such as aluminium sulphate aid this method[25].
Air/steam stripping	Separates organic compounds that are readily vaporised, e.g. VOCs through forced contact with air.

- Secondary Treatment - biological treatment by microorganisms which break down the effluent, which can be aerobic or anaerobic. Anaerobic treatment produces water, hydrogen, hydrogen sulphide, ammonia and volatile fatty acids, which are subsequently broken down into methane and carbon dioxide. Aerobic digestion oxidises the organic material to carbon dioxide and water, while the protein content produces nitrogen oxides and sulphates[25]. Liquid effluent is generally treated aerobically.
- Tertiary Treatment - advanced treatment for the removal of, for example, ammonia, nitrates and phosphates by filtration, settlement, flocculation, ion exchange, ammonia stripping and reed beds. This stage is required for disposal of the effluent to certain watercourses[26].

There is a wide range of treatment methods available for the treatment of effluents and current advances and techniques are reviewed on an annual basis in the journal Water Environment and Research[69].

Technologies are also available for the removal of gases from liquid effluents. These including defoaming techniques, demisting and electrostatic precipitation[70].

Treatment by the water companies/authorities

If the effluent can be discharged to sewer, subject to consents set by the sewerage undertakers and the enforcement agencies, it is treated by the sewerage undertaker. The effluent is received at the treatment plant through the foul sewer.

2.2.3 Gaseous wastes

The amount of information available on gaseous emissions from the food processing industry is variable. While there is not much general data on the types of gaseous emissions, a number of guidelines have been published setting emission limits[74, 75, 76, 77].

Table 10: Summary of the types of gaseous emissions from various food production processes[73]

Process	Typical Emissions (from where)	Control Measures
Meat smoke houses	PM, carbon monoxide, Volatile Organic Compounds (VOCs), polycyclic aromatic hydrocarbons, organic acids, e.g. acetic, formic, propionic, butyric, acrolein, acetaldehyde, formaldehyde, NO_x (smoke)	Afterburners, wet scrubbers, modular electrostatic precipitation.
Meat rendering	VOCs, organic sulphides, disulphides, C4-C7 aldehydes, trimethylamine, C4 amines, quinoline, dimethyl pyrazine, C3-C6 organic acids. Also C4-C7 alcohols, ketones, aliphatic hydrocarbons, aromatic hydrocarbons	Wet scrubbers
Canned fruit and vegetables	PM (solids handling, drying, condensation of vapours), VOCs (cooking stages)	Wet scrubbers, dry sorbants, cyclones
Dehydrated fruits and vegetables	PM (solids handling), VOCs (waste-water treatment ponds), SO_2 (colour preservation)	Scrubbers, sorbents, cyclones
Processed cheese	PM, CO_2 (combustion fuels), VOC (coagulation and ripening stages)	Wet scrubbers, cyclones, fabric filters
Cereals	PM (solids handling), VOCs (thermal processes e.g. drying, steaming, toasting), VOCs (adhesives for packaging)	Fabric filters, wet scrubbers
Corn wet milling	PM (solids handling), hexane (oil extraction), VOCs (grain drying), SO_2 (milling operations)	Ventilation systems, hood systems, cyclones, fabric filters
Pasta manufacturing	PM (solids handling), VOCs (thermal processes)	Cyclones, fabric filters, wet scrubbers

Sugar beet processing	PM, combustion products, VOCs (kilns, stoves, boilers). Also SO_x, NO_x, CO_2, CO, VOCs, ammonium (pulp dryers and evaporators)	Cyclone systems, wet scrubbers, hood systems
Cane sugar processing	PM, combustion products - NO_x, CO, CO_2, SO_x, VOCs (granulators, conveying, packaging, boilers, kilns)	Fabric filters, cyclone systems, wet scrubbers
Almond processing	PM (hulls, shells), VOCs (roasting). Also heavy metal trace contaminants from soils - arsenic, beryllium, cadmium, copper, lead, manganese, mercury, nickel. Concentrations are usually 5×10^{-11} to 5×10^{-4} kg of metal per kg of PM emission. Sources include fertilisers, sprays and groundwater.	Ventilation systems, fabric filters, cyclones.
Coffee roasting	PM, VOCs, organic acids and combustion products. Alcohols, aldehydes, organic acids, nitrogen, sulphur compounds (roasters), CO and CO_2 (combustion products)	Oxidisers (thermal or catalytic)
Fish processing	Smoke, PM. Odours: H_2S, trimethylamine	Afterburners, chlorinator scrubbers or condensers, cyclones
Vegetable oil processing	Hexane (solvent extraction), PM	Cyclones. Hexane is recycled.

The US EPA Office of Air and Radiation (OAR) has produced a publication on emission factors, AP-42[73]. Chapter 9 focuses on the food and drink industries and covers in some detail the various food processes, typical emissions and control measures, which are summarised in Table 10. In some instances there is no information available and not all emissions are controlled. Control methods used in the UK may be different.

Control systems

◆ Cyclone systems - these use the higher inertia of particles to separate them from the gas stream[78].
◆ Wet scrubbers - these are washing devices. The gas is flooded with an aqueous scrubbing liquid which absorbs VOCs[73]. These droplets are then collected[78].
◆ Fabric filters - these are permeable bags which collect particulate matter and allow the gas stream through[78].
◆ Afterburners - odours and fumes are controlled by raising the exhaust temperatures[78].
◆ Catalytic oxidation - eliminates smoke and odours and converts the compounds to CO_2 and H_2O at low temperatures[78].

2.3 Commercial waste

Commercial waste is waste from any trade or business or from any establishment used for recreation or sport. This includes waste from offices or showrooms, hotels, catering establishments, restaurants, businesses, parts of building that are used for domestic and trade purposes and waste from a market or fair[3]. Commercial wastes vary considerably, depending on the type of establishment. Most of these wastes tend to be solid (including food and drink scraps), with the main type of waste being packaging.

2.3.1 Solid wastes

Commercial wastes tend to mirror the types of wastes generated in households and will include food scraps (peelings, waste food, unsold food) and packaging. In 1990, 15 million tonnes of commercial waste[52] was produced in the UK, but this figure has not been broken down into the constituents, therefore it is not possible to determine the amount of food waste that is generated in the commercial sector.

The biggest impact on the commercial sector has been the implementation of packaging waste regulations, set up to promote reuse, recovery and recycling of packaging and reduce the amount disposed to landfill. The large food retailers are making significant moves in the reuse and recycling of packaging materials.

In order to be able to recycle the material, the packaging needs to be designed in order to facilitate the recycling process without compromising food safety or hygiene. Measures include ease of sorting and reprocessability, such that if different plastics are used in one product, both types can be reprocessed together[54]. Another aspect is to minimise the amount of packaging used.

In addition to managing wastes generated through their business activities, retailers also play a major role in recycling household wastes by providing recycling collection points at their locations (Table 11).

Table 11 - The number of recycling banks available at UK supermarkets (1999)[55]

Recycling Units	Total Number of Units
Glass	2,423
Paper	1,160
Metals	1,097
Textiles and shoes	960
Books	283
Plastics	905
Total	6,828

Example - Recycling materials

Tesco's Recycling and Service Units have been established to reclaim recyclable material. Over 160,000 tonnes of used cardboard is converted to plasterboard and other building materials, and 10,000 tonnes of shrink-wrap is being recycled into bin liners. Using plastic product trays will save over 50,000 tonnes of cardboard.

Reference:

Tesco Annual Report and Accounts, 1996. (Reference 53).

Another major waste from the commercial sector is food residuals and unless this waste is separated from the waste stream, it ends up being disposed of to landfill. With the advent of the landfill directive to reduce the amount of biodegradable waste going to landfill, and increasing disposal costs with the landfill tax, measures are now being taken to find alternative disposal methods, such as composting schemes and donating food to the needy.

Litter is a problem that is experienced mainly by the retail sector, especially fast food outlets, although litter on farmland and factory sites, resulting from transport by wind or by fly-tipping (dumping), can occur. Studies by the Tidy Britain Group[58] show that - after smoking related wastes - sweet wrappers, drink containers and fast food packaging are the main litter types.

Various measures such as the Code of Practice on Litter and Refuse[59] and sponsorship schemes for refuse bins by retailers, aim to reduce this problem.

While the large organisations have schemes in place for the management of wastes, smaller establishments also have a role to play in segregating the waste stream to ensure best treatment options. Economies of scale help the larger organisations, but with increasing disposal costs and legislative controls, smaller organisations will have to take measures to minimise their waste and ensure that it is disposed of in an appropriate manner.

Example - Food recovery

In a study completed in the US, recovery of food from consumer, retail and food service sectors, for one year, would "represent the equivalent of a day's food for 4 million people". The San Francisco Produce Recycling Program (EPA-530-F-98-023h) collected more than 60 tonnes of food a month from 25 wholesalers, for 15 months. Food, such as dried, canned and pre-packaged product, was sorted and 37 tonnes a month was sent to charities.

References:

US EPA Office of Solid Waste, "Don't throw that food away", EPA-530-F-98-023 (Reference 56) and "Donating surplus food to the needy", EPA-530-F-96-038 (Reference 57).

Example - Olympic waste

An example of a comprehensive waste control scheme is that to be implemented at the Olympics in 2000 in Sydney, Australia. The organisers have established an integrated waste management scheme to ensure that all of the waste generated is treated in the most appropriate manner to reduce the amounts going to landfill. Each of the waste streams will be segregated. All disposable plates, knives and forks will be composted with the food waste. Drink containers (plastic, metal and paper), where new recycled plastic cups for beer and wine will be used, will be sorted and recycled. Suppliers of food have been asked to minimise all of their packaging and a list of which materials are acceptable (e.g. cardboard, fibre bags, compostable plastics, aluminium and steel cans) or not (e.g. polystyrene, plastic foodware, clingfilm) is given.

References:

Sydney Olympics Games Committee, "Green Games" (Reference 60) and "Integrated Waste Management Solutions - the Strategy for the Sydney 2000 Games" (Reference 61).

2.3.2 Liquid wastes

Liquid effluent from trade/commercial premises should pass into a foul sewer and in some instances a trade effluent consent will be required. Specific measures are required to prevent contaminated water from various washing operations from entering the surface drainage system. These washing operations include:

- Wastewater from trolley, bakery equipment and kitchen cleaning[71].
- Floor and window cleaning[72].
- Cleaning of yard and parking areas[72].
- Discharges from plant rooms, air conditioning and heating systems[72].
- Loading bays[72].

2.3.3 Gaseous waste

Any gaseous wastes tend to be from cooking vents or odours from poor storage of waste food. Good hygienic practices should eliminate odours[79].

The US EPA report on air emissions, AP-42, showed that the vapours released from the frying of chips include particulate matter, oil droplets and water vapour[73].

3. WASTE TREATMENT OPTIONS

This section looks at various options available for treating waste. It describes some basic principles that have become established, before taking a closer look at the options for waste treatment as embodied in the waste management hierarchy - namely minimisation, reuse, recycling and disposal.

There are numerous ways in which waste can be treated. The best method of disposal of any particular waste has to take into account many factors including treatment, transport, energy and environmental costs, and is defined in the concept of Best Practicable Environmental Option (BPEO).

BPEO is "the option which gives the most benefits or least damage to the environment as a whole, at acceptable cost, in the long term as well as the short term"[80]. BPEO takes into account the total pollution from a process and the techniques that are available for dealing with it. The risks of transferring pollutants from one medium to another are also considered (e.g.: solid waste in a landfill will produce landfill leachate and landfill gas when the waste decomposes). The option that is chosen should be one that has an acceptable cost, while causing the least environmental damage and is achieved using Best Available Techniques Not Entailing Excessive Cost (BATNEEC)[81].

BATNEEC was established in the Environment Protection Act 1990 (see Chapter 6) to control emissions to water, air and land. The European equivalent is BAT (Best Available Techniques). The techniques that should be used to control these emissions are those that are the most effective for any particular operation, but any benefits gained should be in relation to the cost of obtaining them; for example, high installation costs cannot be justified on the basis of small reductions in emissions. New industrial plants, as specified in various guidance notes[98], must have the best available techniques installed at the onset, whereas older plants may not be able to justify the costs of implementing these techniques and are therefore not required, under the guidance notes, to have them installed retrospectively[81].

The waste hierarchy (Table 12) was developed to act as a guide to the possible disposal options for a particular waste. While the higher level options are the preferred, some wastes still have to be disposed of by incineration or by depositing in landfills, due to their nature, e.g. the waste may be too hazardous to be recycled and must be incinerated (following the principles set out in BPEO).

Table 12 - Waste Management Hierarchy[27, 82]

Ranking	Treatment/Disposal	Definition
1	Waste minimisation	Limiting the amount of waste produced at source
2	Reuse	Reusing the material for its original purpose
3	Recycling	Involves some reprocessing of the material before it can be used again. Also includes: ● Composting ● Landspreading ● Energy from waste
4	Disposal	Actual removal of the material from the waste stream. Includes: ● Incineration without energy recovery ● Landfill

For a more detailed description of the various waste management and treatment technologies, there are many books that are available on the subject, e.g. "Waste Treatment and Disposal", by P.T. Williams[83].

3.1 Waste minimisation

The aim of minimising waste is to prevent the waste from being produced in the first instance. In order to determine where savings and reductions can be made, all aspects of the manufacturing process need to be investigated and costs and volumes calculated. As each part of the process is investigated, areas where reductions can be made are highlighted and can include, for example:

- Raw material and ingredient use.
- Water consumption and effluent generation.
- Packaging, factory and office consumables.
- Energy consumption[84].

By reducing the amount of raw materials used (e.g. ingredients, water or office consumables) the total waste disposal or waste treatment costs should be reduced. This ultimately saves organisations money.

Example - Reduced packaging

Nestlé Rowntree has developed a new wrapping machine that enables bumper packs of Kit Kat to be wrapped in a single packaging layer. Previously the biscuits also required an inner collation wrap and changes to the process have enabled the amount of polypropylene to be reduced by 100 tonnes per year.

References:

Reducing the cost of packaging in the food and drink industry. ETBPP, GG157. (Reference 85).

There are a number of environmental/green business clubs, such as the Environmental Technology Best Practice Programme (ETBPP) which is government funded, or independent clubs for companies within the same geographic area. These clubs aim to help organisations minimise their waste through providing advice, publishing guides and promoting environmental management systems.

3.2 Reuse

Reuse of a waste product tends to be defined as using the waste in its raw form, without further processing, i.e. the product is recognisable in its original form. Examples include the reuse of milk bottles and transit packaging such as plastic crates instead of cardboard and encouraging the reuse of plastic bags at supermarkets[4].

Example - Fewer carrier bags

The Sainsbury's "Smart Box" scheme, where a sturdy plastic box is used to store and transport customers' shopping, is typical of the scheme used by several major retailers. Sainsbury's estimate that the scheme has reduced carrier bag usage and saves 840 tonnes of plastic per year and that the "Penny Back" scheme (1p paid to customers that reuse carrier bags) has resulted in 75 million bags being reused in 1997/8, saving 900 tonnes of plastic.

References:

Sainsbury's Environmental Report, 1998. (Reference 86)

Reuse does not have to be within the industry or process that generated the original waste material. A number of waste exchanges exist, where organisations provide details of their waste so that it can be traded to another organisation who may regard it as a raw material. This encourages the use of secondary raw materials. Waste exchanges deal with all types of waste and have included food industry wastes. Some recent examples include soya bean lecithin[87], canteen waste and cooking oil[88].

3.3 Recycling

In contrast to reuse, the recycling of any material requires further processing. This may involve break-up of the original material and reforming it into a recognisable product. Examples of this include the recycling of plastic containers, paper and steel[4].

Example - Encouraging use of recycled material

The "Buy Recycled" Campaign, run by Waste Watch and Local Authority Recycling Advisory Committee (LARAC), aims to encourage customers to buy non-food products such as tissue products and refuse sacks, that are made from recycled goods. This scheme is supported by most of the major supermarkets in the UK.

References:

"Sainsbury's aims to kickstart 'Buy Recycled' campaign", for full report see Ends Report No. 296, p34. (Reference 89)

Recycling, therefore, has an impact on the environment, with regard to the energy cost in reprocessing the material and costs for the collection and transport. The current markets for recycled material are poor but schemes to encourage customers to buy recycled products exist.

The use of recycled material helps reduce the amount of raw virgin material that is used. It can help cut energy usage, and reduce air and water emissions in comparison to using raw virgin material. It also reduces the amount of waste going to landfill[27].

3.3.1 Composting

Composting is the natural degradation of organic material by the action of bacteria, fungi, insects and animals in an adequate air supply to reduce it to a stable material which can be used to improve the fertility of soil[90]. Composting can be considered a form of recycling. The resulting material, after the waste has been broken down, is stable and granular and contains plant nutrients. The application of compost to soil improves its structure and can enhance the soil's biological activity[4, 27].

Example - Composted waste

A farm in Lincolnshire is composting food processing waste for use as a fertiliser. Local processing companies are providing fruit and vegetable wastes and the resulting material is used on the land, thereby reducing the amount of manufactured fertiliser used.

References:

"An on-farm way of putting waste to use", Farmer's Weekly, 1996, 5 July, p85. (Reference 91)

Composting is an aerobic process, where bacteria, in the presence of oxygen, break down the biodegradable material. The biodegradable material can also be broken down by bacteria in the absence of oxygen, a process known as anaerobic digestion. The breakdown is accelerated by using enclosed vessels and the resulting mass is used as a fertiliser[92]. Anaerobic digestion has been used for a number of years specifically for the breakdown of hazardous wastes such as sewage sludge and animal slurry and food processing effluents[92].

Another type of composting that is gaining popularity is vermicomposting, where worms, such as *Eisenia foetida*, break down the organic material and the resulting castings are used to produce a fertiliser additive[93].

The problems of composting include the production of odours, spores and liquid effluent, but compost facilities can help significantly to divert organic waste from disposal to landfill[4].

3.3.2 *Landspreading*

Landspreading of waste is an economical and potentially environmentally safe way of dealing with organic wastes, so long as it is properly controlled[4]. Agricultural wastes such as manure, silage effluent, slurry and crop residues can be used as well as by-products from industrial sources, e.g. sewage sludge, paper sludge and food processing wastes.

The spreading of waste on land is controlled by a number of regulations and farmers are required to set up farm waste management plans to demonstrate that they are complying with the Control of Pollution (Silage, Slurry and Agricultural Fuel Oil) Regulations 1991[94]. Agricultural Codes of Practice: Codes of Good Practice for the Protection of Air[12], Soil[15] and Water[16] cover areas such as odour control and process details to minimise the environmental impact.

The spreading of sewage sludge on land is controlled by the Sewage Sludge (Use in Agriculture) Regulations 1989[95] and the associated Code of Practice[96]. These help implement the EC Directive 86/278/EC[97] on sewage sludge use in agriculture and contain a range of measures to protect soil, crop quality, human and animal health and the environment.

3.3.3 Energy from Waste

There are four main ways in which energy can be recovered from waste:

1. The incineration of waste at a waste-to-energy plant
2. Processing wastes as fuel
3. Burning the methane produced from landfills and composting plants
4. Controlled anaerobic digestion of sewage sludge to generate methane[4].

Current waste-to-energy (WTE) facilities either use biological processes to break down the waste to generate methane, which is burnt as a fuel, or the waste is burnt directly at high temperatures. Electricity and/or heat can be generated from burning waste or methane in combined heat and power (CHP) plants[4].

Incinerators are strictly controlled with regards to emissions to air and Integrated Pollution Control (IPC) guidelines have been produced to ensure high environmental and technological standards[98].

3.4 Disposal

3.4.1 Incineration without energy recovery

Modern incinerators can destroy materials rapidly and are used for the destruction of hazardous wastes that are not suitable for disposal to landfill, as well as other types of wastes[4]. Incinerators do not produce methane gases and reduce the volume of waste for final disposal by about 90%[4]. They do not destroy all of the material and the residuals, ash, have to be disposed of to landfill. Also burning of material produces emissions of substances such as hydrogen chloride, hydrogen fluoride, mercury, cadmium, nitrogen oxides, sulphur oxides and dioxins[98]. Stringent measures are in place to control and minimise these emissions to air and land, which are specified in the IPC guidance note on waste incineration[98].

3.4.2 Landfill

Landfill is the most common form of waste disposal facility in the UK. About 80% of municipal waste and 50% of industrial and commercial waste is disposed of in landfills[27]. The recent EC Directive on the landfilling of waste aims to reduce the total amount of waste disposed of in this manner (See section 6.1.4).

Landfills are engineered waste disposal repositories. Measures are in place to reduce the risk of landfill leachate and landfill gas polluting the environment. Some of the sites utilise the methane gas generated by the degrading waste to produce electricity, which can then be sold. Landfills provide a means of reclaiming land, such as quarries, and when the landfill is finally closed, the land can be used for woodland or wetland creation, golf courses and football pitches[99].

3.5 Who disposes of the waste?

While each sector of the food industry produces waste, the waste management industry is involved in the collection and disposal of the generated wastes. The waste management organisation that collects and disposes of the waste and the disposal methods used depend to a large extent on local circumstances.

Large organisations hold contracts directly with waste management contractors to dispose of the waste. On a smaller scale (e.g. small retail establishments, hotels) it is likely that the waste can be collected with the household waste on the waste collection rounds controlled by the local authority. The waste collection and disposal services controlled by local authorities are contracted out to waste management contractors.

The waste hierarchy aims to promote the most environmentally friendly method of disposal. Sometimes the most efficient method of disposal will be the local landfill site or incinerator when transport, sorting and reprocessing costs of recycling are considered. However, to meet with the recycling targets, many waste contractors now operate Material Recycling Facilities (MRFs) to separate the items that are recyclable and dispose of the remaining fraction. While the current MRFs separate out glass, plastics and paper, it is likely that they will move to further segregate the organic fractions of waste for composting.

3.6 Wastewater treatment

For the treatment of wastewater, two options are available:

1. On-site treatment facilities located on the site of the processor in order to reduce the pollutant concentration before discharge to sewer
2. Treatment by the sewerage undertaker - the effluent is discharged to the foul sewer and is treated at the sewage works.

Discharge consents are required from the Environment Agency and/or from the sewerage undertaker, and the costs of disposal are based on the level of pollutants and the volume of wastewater discharged.

On-site treatment can help to reduce disposal costs and with emerging legislation from the EU, sewerage companies may establish tighter controls for discharges to sewer, thereby 'encouraging' on-site treatment. Treating on-site is a more flexible arrangement, as any changes to the process may result in changes to effluent, requiring new discharge consents. In some instances new characteristics of the effluent may not be treatable at the sewerage undertakers[100].

Treatment by a sewerage undertaker has traditionally been the main disposal route for wastewater from the food industry. Sewerage treatment facilities deal with large quantities of wastewater and can maintain standard effluent quality, even with increased load on their treatment facility[100]. Further details about the treatment of wastewater are given in Chapter 2.2.2.

4. WASTE USE WITHIN THE FOOD INDUSTRY

The food industry recycles a large proportion of wastes within the food chain, e.g. waste food for the production of animal feed or for use as a fertiliser on agricultural land. The industry also uses wastes from other industries.

A large proportion of organic waste is disposed of to agricultural land. The disposal is controlled by the Environmental Protection Act 1990, Part II. A licence is not required under the waste management licensing regulations for spreading of certain organic wastes to land (Table 13), as long as certain criteria are met, such as rate of application to the land and recognised benefits of applying the waste, and that authorisation from the enforcement agencies is given[16].

Table 13 - Wastes that can be spread on land that are exempt from waste management licensing[16]

Waste soil or compost

Waste wood, bark or plant matter

Waste food, drink or materials used in or resulting from the preparation of food or drink

Blood and gut contents from abattoirs

Waste lime

Lime sludge from cement manufacturer gas processing

Waste gypsum

Paper waste sludge, waste paper and de-inked paper pulp

Dredgings from any inland waters

Textile waste

Septic tank sludge

Sludge from biological treatment plants

Waste hair and effluent treatment sludge from a tannery

In Scotland, 96% of waste disposed of to land is agricultural waste, with 3% industrial waste, 1% sewage sludge and less than 1% composted waste. It is expected that the levels of sewage sludge and composted waste disposed of to agricultural land will increase[101].

Two non-food industry wastes used within the food industry are sewage sludge and recycled packaging.

4.1 Sewage sludge

Sewage sludge is the residue resulting from the treatment of wastes at a sewage treatment works. In 1996/97, a total of 1,078 thousand tonnes of sewage sludge was produced in the UK, of which 535 thousand tonnes (49.6%) was disposed of to farmland[52]. In 1996, 264 thousand tonnes (24.5%) of sewage sludge was disposed of into the sea, but with sea dumping banned from the end of 1998, alternative disposal routes need to be found. This may result in an increase in sludge applied to farmland.

While the sludge contains high levels of nutrients such as nitrogen and phosphorus[102], which are used to fertilise the soil, the sludge may also contain elements which are toxic or harmful to the environment, e.g. zinc, copper, cadmium, lead, mercury, chromium and pathogenic bacteria[7]. Treatment is therefore required before application of the sludge to land. Tests, under the Code of Practice[96] of applying sewage sludge to agriculture, need to be completed to ensure that the sludge is suitable for landspreading and criteria are set to monitor land suitability, soil capability and fertility, storage and application. ADAS has established guidelines for applications of sewage sludge to agricultural land.

Other products such as milk and dairy products, washings and animal processing wastes are disposed of to land, but the spreading of mammalian meat and bone meal on land is now banned under the Fertiliser (Mammalian Meat and Bone Meal Regulations) 1998[103] as part of the measures to prevent the spread of BSE.

4.2 Recycled packaging

With the increasing promotion of recycling, driven by the packaging waste regulations, one market for recycled plastic and paper and board is for use as packaging for food products.

Table 14 - Typical uses of recycled plastic in food packaging[107]

Recycled plastic	Use
Expanded polystyrene (EPS)	Foam egg cartons
High density polyethylene (HDPE)	Grocery bags
Polyethylene (PE), polypropylene (PP)	Harvest crates
Polyethylene terephthalate (PET)	Baskets for fruit
Regenerated polyethylene terephthalate (RPET)	Drinks bottles

One of the concerns about using recycled packaging, especially plastic, is the possibility of contamination of the foodstuff by the recycled material. Recovered plastics have more chemical contaminants than virgin plastic. This usually derives from absorption of the contaminant into the plastic, e.g. weed killer is absorbed into its plastic container. The plastic is then reused directly or is reprocessed and, if the contaminant has not been removed, there is a risk that the contaminant could migrate from the plastic into the foodstuff[107].

Legislation is in place which applies to the use of recovered plastic in food to protect the consumer, by ensuring that chemical migration does not impair the quality or the safety of the food[107]. Research is in progress to determine the safety of recycled plastics[108].

4.3 Animal feedstuffs

Legislation, guidelines[105] and assurance schemes[106] have established rules and guidance to prevent the spread of disease and contaminants within the food chain, ensuring high quality feedstuffs. However, recent food scares have brought to light the fact that wastes are being fed to animals[104]. While it was recognised that some food processing wastes were already used as animal feed (e.g. peelings and dairy wastes) the scares/scandals have arisen as "non-traditional" wastes are also being used in this manner. Examples include the BSE crisis resulting from cattle being fed protein derived from cattle and sheep; French cattle being fed sewage; and fat from a rendering plant, possibly contaminated with motor oil, being used in feed enabling PCBs and dioxins to enter the food chain in Belgium.

Further measures are likely to be taken to restrict the composition of animal feed. The European Commission is planning a total ban on the use of recycled fat in animal feed and it is likely that the feeding of catering scraps to animals may also be banned[104].

5. ENVIRONMENTAL MANAGEMENT SYSTEMS (EMS)

5.1 Environmental management standards

Environmental management is a process by which businesses can monitor and minimise their impact on the environment. A number of environmental management systems (EMS) are now available for industrial and commercial businesses. The UK was the first to establish an environmental management standard, BS 7750 (now superseded), which assists industry in assessing its environmental impacts and formulating environmental policies and strategies.

The European Community has established the Eco-Management and Audit Scheme (EMAS). This scheme helps companies manage their environmental impact and publicly report on the progress made. The scheme involves setting up an environmental management system so that all activities of a business that have a significant effect on the environment are managed and properly controlled. Accreditation under EMAS is only open to organisations within the EU and the scheme is currently undergoing a review[109].

Example - Environmental reporting

The supermarket retailer Sainsbury's has produced environmental reports. Their latest report (1998) goes into extensive detail about the arisings and disposal of waste streams, energy uses and food sourcing and lists areas where the company is seeking progress as part of a programme of continual improvement.

References:

J Sainsbury plc - 1998 Environment Report. (Reference 86).

The International Standards Organisation has issued the ISO 14000 series (Table 15), which is a family of standards addressing environmental management. Organisations are accredited to ISO14001. These standards provide a strategic approach for environmental management to be implemented into any type of organisation, on a worldwide basis[110].

BS7750 now has been superseded by ISO 14001 and organisations can be accredited under either EMAS and ISO14001, or both. Currently the uptake of either EMAS or ISO 14001 tends to depend on the type of industry; chemical industries have tended to opt for EMAS (28% of companies registering under EMAS are chemical companies), while a large proportion of electrical companies have opted for ISO 14001 (38% of companies registering under ISO14001 are electrical companies). By the end of 1998, only 2% of the total number of companies registering for the ISO standard were from the food products and tobacco manufacturing sector[111] and no food companies were registered for EMAS at the end of 1999.

Table 15 - ISO 14000 Environmental Management Standards[112]

Standard	Description
14000	Guide to Environmental Management Systems: General Guidelines
14001	Environmental Management Systems: Specifications
14010	Guidelines for environmental auditing: general principles
14011	Guidelines for environmental auditing: audit procedures
14012	Guidelines for environmental auditing: qualification criteria for auditors
14020/24	Environmental Labelling
14031/32	Guidelines on Environmental Performance Evaluation
14040/43	Life cycle assessment general principles and practices

The aim of these schemes is to enhance an organisation's ability to attain and measure improvements in environmental performance[113]. These measures are taken at each stage of the production/distribution process, rather than at the end of the process[113]. The overall benefits can include reduced operating costs, increased productivity and improved financial performance[114].

Example - Life cycle analysis

There are over 150 companies within the Unilever Group producing food products, ranging from margarine and tea to ice cream and frozen foods. Areas such as the production of raw materials, manufacture and distribution of goods and the composition of the products were all highlighted as having some environmental impact. While manufacturing has an impact, it was found in the review that the production of raw materials and the consumption of the products had a greater impact on the environment. Life cycle assessment was carried out for key product categories and improvements have been made for tomato sauces and ice cream.

Reference:

Unilever "Foods" (Reference 115)

5.2 Life cycle analysis

Life Cycle Analysis (LCA) comes under ISO 14040 and is the method by which a product can be analysed for its environmental effects, from the production, processes and use to the disposal of the product, for the life of the product, process or service. Inputs and outputs of any process are analysed, so that the results can be compared to other processes. This enables improvements or changes to the system to be introduced[116].

In performing a LCA, it is usual to focus on one part of the process and account for all of the inputs and outputs at that particular point in the process. For example, a nutrient and energy efficiency in agriculture project focussed on the manufacture of fertilisers, plant protection, machinery, transport from the field to the factory and all on-farm activities[117].

It is recognised that the food production system is a large user of energy and natural resources. While packaging is an important aspect, this seems to have been the only area to have undergone significant life cycle study within the food sector and it is recognised that further studies are required[116].

Example - Life cycle analysis of butter packaging

One of the key research areas for the Swedish Institute for Food and Biotechnology (SIK) is the life cycle analysis of food systems. One such study focussed on a butter packaging system, where a new system was needed to fulfil the high quality requirements with least environmental impact. The packaging materials that were studied included greaseproof paper, aluminium and polythene; polypropene with mineral filling; and polyethylene, plastic and paper. It was found that the system containing aluminium and greaseproof paper required significantly higher energy input and caused higher emissions than the other systems. The systems with mineral filling had the least total primary energy demand.

Reference:

Campden & Chorleywood Food Research Association Annual Review 1999, (Reference 118).

6. LEGISLATION AND CODES OF PRACTICE

This chapter gives an introductory overview of the main legislation pertaining to the management and control of wastes, that is relevant to the food industry. The purpose of this section is to illustrate how legislation can bring about changes in attitude to and management of waste and the coverage is limited to EU Directives, UK Acts of Parliament and UK Statutory Instruments, and some codes of practice and guidelines.

The main aim of these legislative controls is to minimise the environmental impact of the disposal of waste - to protect the environment and human health. The items of legislation discussed in the following sections specifically focus on waste management, but other environmental protection regulations, such as the Groundwater Regulations 1998[119], may also affect the disposal of various waste streams.

6.1 European waste legislation

European Community (EC) legislation in relation to waste has been developing since the 1970s[120]. There are various directives, which cover the management of waste, as illustrated by those listed in Table 16.

These Directives have been developed in conjunction with the European Parliament. All member states are required to integrate the provisions set in the Directives into national legislation, usually within 2 years of them being adopted.

The directives outlined here all have some impact on the food industry. There are other environmental regulations, not mentioned here, which have some bearing on the way the food industry manages its impact on the environment. There are several environmental law guides that cover the legislation in greater detail[121, 122], and these and the legislation itself should be consulted for guidance on specific points.

Table 16: Some EC Directives on Waste Management

Waste Theme	Subject of directives	Directive Number
Waste Management	● Waste	● 75/442/EEC (amended by 91/156/EEC)
	● Hazardous waste	● 91/689/EEC
Waste Treatment and Disposal	● Hazardous waste incineration	● 94/67/EC
	● Landfilling of waste	● 1999/31/EC
Waste Products	● Disposal of waste oils	● 75/439/EEC
	● Disposal of PCBs and PCTs	● 96/59/EC
	● Batteries and accumulators containing certain dangerous substances	● 91/157/EEC
	● Packaging waste	● 94/62/EC
Waste Emissions	● Waste from titanium dioxide industry	● 78/176/EEC
	● Sewage sludge use in agriculture	● 86/278/EEC

Note: This list is illustrative and not intended as a comprehensive list. Other directives, not listed here, may also be applicable and some of those listed may have been amended

6.1.1 Integrated Pollution Prevention and Control

The "Council Directive 96/61/EC of 24 September 1996 concerning integrated pollution prevention and control"[123] sets out measures to prevent, reduce and eliminate pollution at the source of the pollutant and to ensure sensible management of natural resources. These provisions should enable a move towards a sustainable balance between human activity and the environment's resources and regenerative capacity. The overall aim of this directive is to bring about accountability through the "polluter pays" principle[123], where "environmental costs are borne by those directly responsible for any environmental damage"[4].

The directive covers emissions to air, soil and water and while it refers to traditional heavy industries, such as chemical and metal processing industries, the provisions also relate to the following food related activities:

◆ Slaughterhouses (with carcass production capacity at greater than 50 tonnes per day).
◆ Treatment and processing intended for the production of food products from:
   a) Raw animal materials other than milk (production capacity 75 tonnes per day)
   b) Vegetable raw materials (production capacity 300 tonnes per day).
◆ Treatment and processing of milk (quantity of milk received greater than 200 tonnes per day).
◆ Installations for the disposal or recycling of animal carcasses and animal waste with a treatment capacity of over 10 tonnes per day.
◆ Installations for intensive rearing of poultry or pigs with more than:
   a) 40000 places for poultry
   b) 2000 places for production pigs (over 30kg)
   c) 750 places for sows[123].

The Directive allows the use of "Best Available Techniques" (BAT) which balances the cost of installing pollution prevention measures with the overall environmental benefit.

The UK Parliament passed the Pollution Prevention and Control Act in July 1999[124], enacting the terms of the Directive. The provisions are set to be phased in over eight years[125]. The explanatory notes to the Act state that while most of the requirements for industries listed in the Directive are already covered by various parts of the Environmental Protection Act 1990, "a significant number of installations are at present unregulated. This category mainly comprises large intensive pig and poultry installations, plus large installations for the manufacture of food and drink products."[126]. The food and milk industries will be brought under the IPPC regulation by 2002; intensive poultry farming by 2003; and intensive pig rearing by 2004[125].

6.1.2 Packaging waste

The formal title of this Directive is "European Parliament and Council Directive 94/62/EC of 20 December 1994 on packaging and packaging waste"[127]. It aims to harmonise national measures and to minimise the environmental impact of packaging and packaging waste. The objective is to prevent the production of packaging waste and to encourage reuse, recycling and recovery of existing packaging to reduce the amount for final disposal. The UK regulations were passed in 1997 (see Section 6.3.2).

Table 17 - Definitions of reuse, recycling and recovery[128]

Operation	Definition
Reuse	Packaging that has been designed for a minimum number of trips or rotations. It is refilled or used for the same purpose that it was designed for - examples include pallets, carrier bags.
Recycling	Reprocessing of the waste materials for the original purpose or for other purposes.
Recovery	Recovery of specific chemicals or compounds from the waste material - for example solvent reclamation, metal recovery, oil recovery, spreading on land to benefit agriculture.

The targets for recovery and recycling have been set by the EU as:

♦ 50-60% by weight of packaging waste to be recovered and
♦ 25-45% to be recycled.

These targets have to be met within 5 years of the Directive being implemented into national law and applies to the following activities: industrial, commercial, office, shop, service industries and households.

6.1.3 Hazardous waste

The "Council Directive 91/689/EEC of 12 December 1991 on hazardous waste"[129] and "94/904/EC: Council Decision of 22 December 1994 establishing a list of hazardous wastes pursuant to Article 1(4) of Council Directive 91/689/EEC"[130] identify a range of wastes with particular hazardous properties which require special treatment for disposal. The origin and the composition, including the concentration values, of the waste play a part in determining the hazard classification. Food related waste that is designated as hazardous is agrochemical waste.

6.1.4 Landfill

The "Council Directive 1999/31/EC of 26 April 1999 on the landfill of waste"[131] has only recently been passed by the European Parliament and has to be incorporated into UK Law by 2001. One of the main aims of this directive is to reduce the amount of biodegradable municipal waste going to landfill to 35% of the 1995 biodegradable municipal waste arisings. In the UK, 29 million tonnes of municipal waste was disposed of in 1995 and it is presumed that approximately 60% of municipal waste is biodegradable. The figures for the actual amount of biodegradable waste disposed of in 1995 and previous years are not available[132].

The Directive focuses on municipal (i.e. commercial and domestic) waste and while it may not have a direct effect on the industrial processing side of the food industry, it could result in more composted waste being used by the agricultural sector. The Government has recently issued a number of consultation papers to set up a waste management strategy for England and Wales. Specific mention has been made for farmers receiving guidance on the use of compost on agricultural land[27, 133]. The main effect of the Landfill Directive (apart from changes to household waste collection) will be on retailers and caterers, who will have to divert their biodegradable waste from their main waste streams, in order for it to be processed separately.

6.2 UK legislation

The main Act for environmental safeguards is the Environmental Protection Act 1990. This Act brought about substantial changes to UK environment law[121]. It covers a wide range of topics including Integrated Pollution Control (IPC), waste, radioactive substances, genetically modified organisms and nature conservation. The Environment Act 1995 established the environmental enforcement agencies and expanded environmental law to cover areas such as contaminated land and air quality.

6.2.1 Environmental Protection Act 1990[1]

Part I of the Act covers Integrated Pollution Control (IPC), establishes the use of BATNEEC (Best Available Techniques Not Entailing Excessive Costs) to achieve the Best Practicable Environmental Option (BPEO)[121] and divides the responsibility for monitoring and enforcing pollution control between the local authorities and government departments. Heavy industrial sectors, such as metal foundries, and chemical and petrochemical processors, are under the control of the government departments, while "lighter" industrial sectors such as vegetable oil and fish oil processing[74, 75, 76] are under the control of the local authorities.

Part II of the Act covers waste on land. It:

♦   Establishes provisions for prohibiting the harmful treatment or disposal of waste
♦   Sets up the Duty of Care Code of Practice

- Establishes the waste management licensing regime, whereby a licence is required for treatment, storing or disposal of controlled waste
- Gives provisions for the collection, disposal or treatment of controlled waste and
- Recognises the requirements of special and non-controlled waste.

Integrated Pollution Control (IPC) and BATNEEC are similar principles to Integrated Pollution Prevention and Control (IPPC) and BAT, set up in the IPPC Directive. Although not all industries covered by IPPC are covered by IPC, due to the similarities between the two systems, the introduction of IPPC would not significantly change current UK practice[121].

While the Act itself introduces the various measures, the specific details of the measures are defined in individual Statutory Instruments.

6.2.2 Environment Act 1995[2]

This Act made several amendments to the Environmental Protection Act 1990. One of the key provisions was the establishment of enforcement agencies:

- England and Wales - the Environment Agency
- Scotland - Scottish Environmental Protection Agency (SEPA).

These Agencies were made up from specific divisions from the then Department of the Environment: Her Majesty's Inspectorate of Pollution (HMIP), the National Rivers Authority (NRA) and the Waste Regulation Authorities. These enforcement agencies took over the government regulation of the IPC processes.

The Act defines the functions, rights, powers and duties of the Agencies for the "purpose of preventing or minimising, or remedying or mitigating the effects of pollution of the environment"[2].

The Act also enables legislation on producer responsibility to be passed. The aim of producer responsibility legislation is "for the purpose of promoting or securing an increase in the reuse, recovery or recycling of products or materials"[2].

6.3 Some key statutory instruments

In addition to the primary Acts described above, many Statutory Instruments (SIs) impinge on waste management in the UK and a small selection of SIs are discussed briefly below. Note that these are covered for illustrative purposes and should not be regarded as a definitive guide to the law. More extensive reference works and the legislation itself should be consulted for further guidance. The references below are to the original SIs, but these are constantly changing and it is necessary to refer to the amendments.

6.3.1 Special Waste Regulations

These regulations[134] set out provisions for the keeping, treatment or disposal of controlled wastes that are dangerous or difficult to manage[135]. The regulation implements the Hazardous Waste Directive (91/689/EEC)[129] and incorporates the Hazardous Waste Listing (91/904/EC)[130], as well as expanding the list to include other hazardous wastes[135].

These regulations establish a system to manage the wastes from the moment that they are produced until final disposal or recovery[135]. The enforcement agencies are required to be notified of any movement or disposal of special wastes. An overall indication of whether a waste could be classed as special includes wastes that are: explosive, oxidising, flammable, irritant, harmful, toxic, carcinogenic, corrosive, infectious, teratogenic, mutagenic, release toxic gases on reaction, form hazardous products after disposal or are ecotoxic[135]. Examples of food processing wastes which could be classified as special as detailed in the Special Waste Regulations Joint Circular are given in Table 18. To define a waste as special requires knowledge of various properties of the waste, the details of which go beyond the scope of this publication, but further guidance can be obtained from the Special Wastes Technical Guidance Note[159].

Table 18 - Food processing wastes which could be classified as special[135]

Category	Sources
Primary production wastes	• Sludges from washing and cleaning • Animal tissue waste • Plant tissue waste • Waste plastics (excluding packaging) • Agrochemical wastes (listed in the Hazardous Waste Listing) • Animal faeces, urine and manure (including spoiled straw)
Wastes from the preparation and processing of meat, fish and other foods of animal origin	• Sludges from washing and cleaning • Animal tissue waste • Materials unsuitable for consumption or processing • Sludges from on-site effluent treatment
Wastes from fruit, vegetables, cereals, edible oils, cocoa, coffee and tobacco preparation, processing; conserve production; tobacco processing	• Sludges from washing, cleaning, peeling, centrifuging and separation • Wastes from preserving agents • Wastes from solvent extraction • Materials unsuitable for consumption or processing • Sludges from on-site effluent treatment
Wastes from sugar processing	• Soil from cleaning and washing beet • Off-specification calcium carbonate • Sludges from on-site effluent treatment
Wastes from the dairy products industry	• Materials unsuitable for consumption or processing • Sludges from on-site effluent treatment
Wastes from the baking and confectionery industry	• Materials unsuitable for consumption or processing • Wastes from preserving agents • Sludges from on-site effluent treatment
Wastes from the production of alcoholic and non alcoholic beverages (excluding coffee, tea and cocoa)	• Wastes from washing, cleaning and mechanical reduction of the raw material • Wastes from spirits distillation • Waste from chemical treatment • Materials unsuitable for consumption or processing • Sludges from on-site effluent treatment

6.3.2 Packaging Waste

This is the first item of legislation under the 'producer responsibility' umbrella and has a big impact on various sectors of the food industry. These regulations require the producer of the waste to "take reasonable steps to recover and recycle packaging waste"[128]. These obligations are to enable the UK to meet the recovery and recycling targets set out in the Directive 94/62/EC on packaging and packaging waste (see Section 6.1.2).

Producers are required to register either with the enforcement agencies or with one of a number of registered schemes, if they meet the following requirements: 50 tonnes of packaging waste produced per year, and a turnover of over £2 million[136]. Producers include manufacturers, converters, packer/fillers, importers, wholesalers and sellers and the waste includes packaging and transit packaging material[128].

As a result of the DETR consultation to amend the 1997 regulations, changes will be made to the percentage obligations for recovered material and the threshold levels, and the system will be simplified[136].

6.3.3 Landfill Tax

These regulations[137] were brought in to reduce the volume of waste disposed of to landfill and to encourage recycling of waste products. The current rate of landfill tax is £10 per tonne of waste and £2 per tonne for inert wastes (such as rubble), but these levels are expected to rise. Some of the revenue collected through this tax is earmarked for environmental projects[138].

Example - Earmarked landfill tax

The Nottinghamshire Wildlife Trust has built new headquarters funded from landfill tax earmarked for such projects. It includes an exhibition area to provide further information about conservation issues and projects, and the local children will develop a library and garden area.

Reference:

ENTRUST - Achievement Brochure. (Reference 138)

6.3.4 Animal by-products

This Order covers the treatment and disposal of animal by-products. Areas covered include:

- carcasses
- products of animal origin
- catering waste (including domestic waste)
- wastes from the production of products which are intended to be used for human consumption without further cooking
- waste from the production of bread, cakes, pasta, pastry, pizzas and similar products[139].

In order to minimise the risk of spreading diseases to other animals and man, certain provisions are laid out regarding the disposal of animal by-products. These restrictions affect rendering and incineration plants and the feeding of catering wastes to pigs and poultry[139].

6.4 Wastewater legislation

The main Acts of Parliament for the control of water are the Water Resources Act 1991[140] and the Water Industry Act 1991[141]. There are a number of Statutory Instruments that apply to the treatment and disposal of industrial wastewater.

The Water Resources Act covers various provisions regarding water management. One section in the Act, for example, covers pollution and pollution offences, specifically highlighting codes of good agricultural practice[140]. Discharges into public sewers are also detailed and the release of polluting substances is specifically prohibited, Table 19.

Table 19 - The listing of chemicals with restrictions of disposal to sewer - the Red List[142]

Mercury and its compounds	1,2-Dichloroethane
Cadmium and its compounds	Trichlorobenzene
Gamma-hexachlorocyclohexane	Atrazine
DDT	Simazine
Pentachlorophenol and its compounds	Tributyltin compounds
Hexachlorobenzene	Triphenyltin compounds
Hexachlorobutadiene	Trifluralin
Aldrin	Fenitrothion
Dieldrin	Azinphos-methyl
Endrin	Malathion
Carbon tetrachloride	Endosulfan
Polychlorinated biphenyls	Trichloroethylene (added in 1992 amendment)[121]
Dichlorvos	Perchloroethylene (added in 1992 amendment)[121]

The Water Industry Act 1991 covers discharge consents and charges. It defines trade effluent as "any liquid that is wholly or partly produced in the course of any trade or industry carried on at a trade premises" and sets out the provisions for the disposal of the effluent, i.e. the implementation of discharge consents[141].

Both of these Acts are further amended by the Environment Act 1995, through establishing the enforcement of the regulations through the Environment Agency and SEPA.

6.4.1 Trade Effluents

This regulation[142] sets specific controls for the discharge of effluent which contains the Red List chemicals (Table 19). Controls are also required for the discharge of effluent from the manufacture of paper pulp, asbestos cement and asbestos paper or board, or production of chlorinated organic chemicals[121].

In order to dispose of this effluent, consent must be obtained from the sewerage undertaker. The enforcement agencies need to be informed of the discharge if the effluent contains Red List chemicals or is from the specified industries[121].

6.4.2 Urban Waste Water Treatment Regulations

These regulations allow for modification of the discharge consents by the sewerage undertakers[143]. Also, a list of industries is given whose discharges will be specifically controlled by the enforcement agencies on and after 31st December 2000[143, 144].

Table 20 - List of industries where discharge will come under the enforcement agency control on 31/12/2000[143].

Milk processing

Manufacture of fruit and vegetable products

Manufacture and bottling of soft drinks

Potato processing

Meat industry

Breweries

Production of alcohol and alcoholic beverages

Manufacture of animal feed from plant products

Manufacture of gelatin and glue from hides, skin and bones

Malt-houses

Fish-processing industry

The Government has issued a number of consultation papers in order to establish a strategy for managing waste in England and Wales, building on the previous Government's White Paper "Making Waste Work"[4]. This will result in the development of further legislation and guidelines.

Separate legislation is also available for Scotland and Northern Ireland, and may contain different provisions. With the advent of devolved powers in Scotland and Wales, further legislation for the protection of the environment, specific to those regions, is likely to emerge.

6.5 Codes of practice and guidelines

There are numerous codes of practice available to help industry minimise its impact on the environment. The main code of practice relating to waste management is the Duty of Care[145]. The Duty of Care applies to any person who produces, imports, carries, keeps, treats or disposes of controlled waste. The persons concerned must ensure that the waste is dealt with in a proper and safe manner. The Duty of Care

Code of Practice describes a series of steps which should help users meet the Duty. It is a legal obligation to comply with the Duty of Care (as set out in subsection 34(1) of the Environmental Protection Act 1990)[145].

Some examples of other Codes of Practice are detailed below.

6.5.1 Codes of Practice for Agriculture

A set of four codes of practice has been issued by MAFF for agriculture. These guides (for the protection of air[12], soil[15], water[16] and for the management of agricultural and horticultural waste[17]) cover legal issues, treatment, storage and management of various wastes. They provide, for example, guidelines for disposal (e.g. required distances from watercourses), advise on siting of slurry stores and steps for reducing the emissions of greenhouse gases.

6.5.2 Pollution Prevention Guidelines (PPGs)

Produced by the Environment Agency, SEPA and the Environment and Heritage Service, these guidelines focus on various pollution risks. They contain general and basic legal information, highlight possible pollutants and identify risks associated with the pollutants and preventative measures. Some of those applicable to the food industry include:

- The prevention of pollution of controlled waters by pesticides - PPG9[146]
- Dairies and other milk handling operations - PPG17[147]

Copies of these guidelines and a full listing of those available can be found on the SEPA and Environment Agency websites.

6.5.4 *Integrated Pollution Control Guidelines*

The Integrated Pollution Control guidelines first originated as Her Majesty's Inspectorate of Pollution (HMIP) Process Guidance notes and are currently being revised by the Environment Agency. The guides provide general information on processes and technical information on measures to limit environmental impact. Although these focus on heavy industrial processes, specific guidance is given about the combustion of meat and bonemeal, and the combustion of animal carcasses, resulting from measures to prevent the spread of BSE infected material[148, 149]. With the implementation of the Pollution Prevention and Control Act, new guidelines focussing on BAT techniques for the food industry are currently being produced. The European Integrated Pollution Prevention and Control Bureau aims to set up BAT guidance notes for the industries that do not already have them within the next five years[150].

7. SOURCES OF INFORMATION

Environmental information, not just that pertaining to waste, is found in a wide range of document types and includes books, journals, reports and newsletters and, more and more, the Internet.

The following sections give details of information sources covering legislation, guidance and publications for all aspects of the environment. The sources quoted cover all types of industry, not just the food and drink industry - in many cases this will need to be borne in mind as information relating to the food and drink industry has to be extracted from the document which has wider relevance.

7.1 Legislation

Direct access to UK Statutory Instruments and to the European Community Official Journals can be obtained via the legislation section on the CCFRA website at www.campden.co.uk

7.1.1 UK Legislation

◆   Acts of Parliament and Statutory Instruments
    UK Acts of Parliament and Statutory Instruments, published since 1997, are available free of charge over the Internet, from www.hmso.gov.uk or are available from www.ukstate.com   Items published prior to 1997 can be purchased from The Stationery Office, 123 Kingsway, London WC2B 6PQ. Tel: 020 7242 6393. Fax: 020 7242 6412.

♦ UK Codes of Practice

Some of these are free but others may be charged. Most of the chargeable publications are available from The Stationery Office website at www.itsofficial.net.

A list of the Integrated Pollution Control (IPC) Guidance notes is available on the Environment Agency website, with full bibliographic details. This can be found at www.environment-agency.gov.uk/epns/ipchome.html.

Free publications are available from the organisations that authored them (e.g. Department of Environment Transport and the Regions (DETR) consultation papers are available directly from the DETR) and more are now being made available over the Internet.

Pollution Prevention Guidelines are available from www.environment-agency.gov.uk/epns/ppgs.html.

Agricultural Pollution Prevention Leaflets are available from www.sepa.org.uk/publications/pubhome.htm.

♦ Consultation Papers

Most are available from the relevant government websites such as www.detr.gov.uk or www.environment-agency.gov.uk or www.sepa.org.uk They are also available in hard copy from the DETR Free Literature Service tel: 0870 122 6236, or the Environment Agency tel: 0645 333111.

It may be necessary to contact specific departments of the DETR if the consultation is highly specialised.

7.1.2 European Legislation

European legislation is published in the Official Journal (OJ). This is available on the Europa website where it is held for 45 days post publication, europa.eu.int/eur-lex/en/oj/index.html

A listing of current directives in force, with direct links to their full text, can be found at europa.eu.int/eur-lex/en/lif/ind/en_analytical_index_15.html

7.1.3 US Legislation

US legislation is published in the Federal Register at www.epa.gov/fedrgstr

7.2 Environmental guides

These tend to be subscription services, with updates issued every three months or
so. Croner Publications Ltd publish a wide range of guides such as:

- Croner's Waste Management (containing legislation, handling and disposal
  information of certain wastes, directory of companies)
- Croner's Environmental Policy and Procedures (containing details of
  environmental management systems).

Further details of guides are available at www.croner.co.uk or from Croner
Publications Ltd, Croner House, London Road, Kingston upon Thames, Surrey, KT2
6SR. UK. Tel: +44 (0) 20 8547 3333 Fax: +44 (0) 20 8547 2637.

In addition to these examples, there are many books summarising the current state
of UK environmental legislation.

7.3 Statistics and data

Government publications such as the Digest of Environmental Statistics are
available from The Stationery Office and on the Internet at
www.environment.detr.gov.uk/des20/index.htm. A free pocket guide is available
from the DETR Free Literature Service (tel: 0870 122 6236).

7.4 Databases

A wide range of environmental databases is available. These are bibliographic
databases in that the information provided includes authors, publication title and full
bibliographic details to enable readers to get hold of the item. Most contain an
abstract, summarising the content of the document.

These databases are available on CD-ROM and/or on database hosts. Database hosts hold a wide range of databases on all subjects and allow subscribers to search them. Hosts do not produce the databases, they simply provide convenient access to databases compiled by other organisations. Generally users need to have an account with the database hosts before searching the database, but this situation is changing. Service organisations such as CCFRA hold accounts with the database hosts and can search the databases on your behalf, subject to current copyright laws.

General environmental databases include Enviroline, which covers environmental design and energy, and Pollution Abstracts, which covers noise, wastewater treatment and toxicology. Both cover pollution of land, air and water.

Two specialised databases are:

♦ WasteInfo - which contains details of publications on the policies and economics of waste management, as well as information on waste minimisation, reuse, recycling and the various treatment and disposal options.

♦ Aqualine - which contains information on water. It covers water resources, water quality, analysis and monitoring, treatment and industrial effluents.

Further details about environmental databases are available from, for example:

Dialog who publish databases and provide information sheets on these. Details can be viewed at library.dialog.com/bluesheets/html/blf.html or contact Dialog at: Dialog Corporation, The Communications Building, 48 Leicester Square, London, WC2H 7DB, UK. Tel: +44 (0) 20 7930 6900. Fax: +44 (0) 20 7930 6006.

SilverPlatter who publish databases on CD-ROM. Details can be viewed at www.silverplatter.com or contact Silverplatter at: SilverPlatter Information Ltd, Merlin House, 20 Belmont Terrace, Chiswick, London, W4 5UG. Tel: +44 (0) 20 8585 6400. Fax: +44 (0) 20 8585 6640.

Questel Orbit - a database host. Details can be viewed at www.questel.orbit.com or contact Questel Orbit at: Questel Orbit, 4, rue des Colonnes, 75082 Paris Cedex 02, France. Telephone: +33 (0) 1 55 04 52 00. Facsimile: +33 (0) 1 55 04 52 01

In addition to those listed there are various other database hosts and environmental databases available.

7.5 Reports

R&D reports have been published by the then Department of the Environment and now by the Environment Agency, covering all areas of the environment. These are now sold by the Environment Agency R&D Dissemination Centre at WRc plc. A full listing is available on the WRc website at www.wrcplc.co.uk/rdbookshop and on a free CD-ROM from Environment Agency R&D Dissemination Centre, WRc plc, Blagrove, Swindon, Wiltshire SN5 8YF. Tel: +44 (0) 1793 865138. Fax: +44 (0) 514562.

7.6 Other sources

7.6.1 Government

♦   **Environment Agency for England and Wales**
    Environment Agency, Rio House, Waterside Drive, Aztec West, Almondsbury, Bristol, BS32 4UD. Tel: +44 (0) 1454 624400. Fax: +44 (0) 1454 624409. www.environment-agency.gov.uk

♦   **Scottish Environment Protection Agency (SEPA)**
    Scottish Environmental Protection Agency (SEPA), Erskine Court, The Castle Business Park, Stirling, FK9 4TR. Tel: +44 (0) 1786 457700. Fax: +44 (0) 1786 446885. www.sepa.org.uk

- **DETR - The Department of Environment, Transport and the Regions**
  Department of Environment, Transport and the Regions (DETR), Eland House, Bressenden Place, London, SW1E 5DU. Tel: +44 (0) 20 7890 3000. www.detr.gov.uk

- **Scottish Executive Rural Affairs Department**
  Scottish Executive Rural Affairs Department, Pentland House, 47 Robb's Loan, Edinburgh EH14 1TY. Tel: +44 (0) 131 556 8400. www.scotland.gov.uk

- **Department of Agriculture and Rural Development**
  Department of Agriculture and Rural Development, Dundonald House, Upper Newtownards Road, Belfast BT4 3SB, Northern Ireland, U.K. Tel. +44 (0) 28 9052 4999. Fax. +44 (0) 28 9052 5003. www.dani.gov.uk/index.htm

- **ENVIRONMENT (was DGXI)**
  This is the site for the Department of the Environment, Civil Protection and Nuclear Safety in the EU: europa.eu.int/comm/environment/index_en.htm

- **EEA**
  European Environment Agency site contains information on the environment at the European level and can be found at eea.eu.int

- **US EPA - Office of Solid Waste and Emergency Response**
  US Environmental Protection Agency (US EPA), Office of Solid Waste, RCRA Information Center, 401 M Street, SW, Washington DC 20460. www.epa.gov

7.6.2 Specialist Organisations

◆ **Aqualine**. Run by WRc plc, Aqualine provides information on all issues related to water. A helpline is available. The Aqualine database is available through database hosts, on CD-ROM and in hard copy.

WRc plc, AQUALINE, Frankland Road, Blagrove, Swindon SN5 8YF. Tel: 01793 865000. Fax: 01793 865001.

◆ **CADDET**. Split into two areas covering Energy Efficiency and Renewable Energy, CADDET is an international body that gathers information on full-scale commercial projects which are operating in member countries.

CADDET Energy Efficiency, ETSU, Harwell, Didcot, Oxfordshire, OX11 0BR. www.caddet-ee.org
CADDET Centre for Renewable Energy, ETSU, 168 Harwell, Didcot, Oxfordshire, OX11 0RA. www.caddet-re.org

◆ **Environment Technology Best Practice Programme** (ETBPP) provides help and advice on waste minimisation and provides a free consultancy service. A whole series of guides are available and a complete listing is available on the website etbpp.netgates.co.uk

Environmental Helpline: 0800 585794

◆ **Waste Management Information Bureau** (WMIB). Run by AEA Technology Environment and currently funded by the DETR, WMIB provides information and advice on all aspects of non-nuclear waste management. It publishes the WasteInfo database (available through database hosts and on CD-ROM) and runs a helpline service.

Waste Management Information Bureau, AEA Technology Environment, F6 Culham, Abingdon, Oxfordshire, OX14 3ED. Tel: 01235 463162. Fax: 01235 463004. Email: wmib@aeat.co.uk

Environmental Services on the Internet

◆ EDIE - Environmental Data Interactive Exchange is a communications service on environmental issues. Registration (free) is required to obtain news items, details of conferences and new publications: www.edie.net

◆ Envirosearch - run by The Stationery Office, it has direct links to over 200 environmental websites. Registration (free) is required www.envirosearch.co.uk

8. CONCLUSIONS

This book set out to review waste issues of relevance to the food industry. It reviews the production, management and disposal of waste along the food production chain - from agriculture, through manufacturing and processing, to retail and food service operations - to illustrate the types of waste that are generated, the way in which these wastes are disposed of and the options and controls that need to be addressed. The waste management hierarchy is of particular significance in this respect. This sets out a basic philosophy and approach of identifying the best disposal options for solid waste. The approach itself reflects the broad trend of initiatives at global, national and local levels: prevent the waste being formed where at all possible, and, when waste is generated, apply consistent criteria to ensure its reuse or disposal has minimal environmental impact.

The general political and social impetus of the management of wastes is becoming established in regulatory controls, as illustrated by the regulatory framework for the EU and the UK. In parallel, quality management systems are emerging to facilitate structured and consistent approaches to environmental management issues. The legislation and quality systems are, therefore, acting respectively as the driver and facilitator, for the food and allied industries to address environmental issues. The food industry needs to recognise its responsibilities in the creation and management of waste materials and ensure responsible reuse where appropriate. To achieve this the industry needs more detailed information and practical guidance. Although these are beyond the scope of this introductory book, further information on these and other environmental issues can be obtained from the section on sources of information and from the extensive references to further reading.

REFERENCES AND FURTHER READING

Note that for references to websites the date of publication is not always apparent. For this reason the citation generally includes 'nd' (no date) for the date of publication though the date on which the website was accessed is stated.

1   UK Parliament, 1990, "Environmental Protection Act 1990". HMSO: London. ISBN: 0105443905.

2   UK Parliament, 1995, "Environment Act 1995". HMSO: London. ISBN: 0105425958.

3   UK Parliament, 1992, "The Controlled Waste Regulations 1992", Statutory Instrument 1992 No. 588. HMSO: London. ISBN: 0110235886.

4   Department of the Environment and Welsh Office, 1995, "Making Waste Work - A Strategy for Sustainable Waste Management in England and Wales", Cm3040. HMSO: London. ISBN: 0101304021.

5   Anon, 1999, "Signs of life in the slow moving world of waste policy". Ends Report, No. 294, p22-26.

6   SEPA, 1997, "Agriculture Leaflet: Diffuse Pollution and Agriculture". SEPA: Stirling. Also available from www.sepa.org.uk

7   Scottish Office Agriculture, Environment and Fisheries Department, 1997, "Prevention of Environmental Pollution from Agricultural Activity - Code of Good Practice". Scottish Office: Stirling.

8   Ministry of Agriculture Fisheries and Food, 1998, "Farm Waste Management Plan - A Step by Step Guide for Farmers". MAFF: London.

9   SEPA, 1997, "Agriculture Leaflet: Disposal of Agricultural Waste Products and Animal Carcasses". SEPA: Stirling. Also available from www.sepa.org.uk

10   SEPA, 1997, "Agriculture Leaflet: Slurry". SEPA: Stirling. Also available from www.sepa.org.uk

11   UK Parliament, 1993, "Clean Air Act 1993". HMSO: London. ISBN:
      0105411930.

12   Ministry of Agriculture, Fisheries and Food, 1998, "The Air Code - Code of
      Good Agricultural Practice", PB 0618. MAFF: London.

13   BDB Associates and Environment Agency, 1996, "Agricultural Waste
      Minimisation". R&D Technical Report Summary P21. Available from
      www.environment-agency.gov.uk Accessed: November 1999.

14   BOC Foundation, ADAS and MAFF, 1997, "Waste Minimisation on Farms".
      Project 5 1997. Available from
      www.boc.com/foundation/projects/proj5_97.htm Accessed: 12/11/99.

15   Ministry of Agriculture, Fisheries and Food, 1998, "The Soil Code - Code of
      Good Agricultural Practice", PB 0617. MAFF: London.

16   Ministry of Agriculture, Fisheries and Food, 1998, "The Water Code - Code of
      Good Agricultural Practice", PB 0587. MAFF: London.

17   Ministry of Agriculture, Fisheries and Food, 1998, "Code of Practice for the
      Management of Agricultural and Horticultural Waste", PB 3580. MAFF:
      London.

18   Dunstone J., Cefaratti P., 1995, "Waste not, want not". Food Manufacture,
      70(3), p48-49.

19   Bioresource Technology. Elsevier Science: Netherlands. ISSN: 09608524.

20   Water Environment Research. Water Environment Federation: USA. ISSN:
      10614303.

21   Water Science and Technology. Elsevier Science: Netherlands. ISSN:
      02731223.

22   Moon N.J., 1980, "Maximising efficiencies in the food system: a review of
      alternatives for waste abatement". Journal of Food Protection, **43**(3), p231-238.

23   Loehr R.C., 1974, "Agricultural Waste Management - Problems, Processes, Approaches". Academic Press Inc: London. ISBN: 0124552501.

24   Hills J.S., 1995, "Cutting Water and Effluent Costs", 2nd Edition. IChemE: Rugby. ISBN: 0852953615.

25   Mead G.C. (ed), 1989, "Processing of Poultry". Elsevier Science Publishers Ltd: Essex. ISBN: 1851663053.

26   Amos P.W., 1997, "Wastewater in the food industry: a review of procedure and practice". Paper from Proceedings of IFST Scottish Branch Workshop - The Importance of Water in the Food Industry. In: Food Science and Technology Today, 11(2), p96-104.

27   Department of Environment, Transport and the Regions, 1999, "A Way with Waste - A Draft Waste Strategy for England and Wales", 99EP02541/2. DETR: London. Also available at www.environment.detr.gov.uk

28   CADDET, 1994, "Anaerobic Digestion of Piggery Waste in Victoria, Australia". CADDET Technical Brochure No.4. Also available from www.caddet-re.org

29   CADDET, 1995, "Poultry Litter Power Station in the United Kingdom". CADDET Technical Brochure No. 17. Also available from www.caddet-re.org

30   Anon, 1999, "Is scrap metal waste?". Industrial Environmental Management, December, p7.

31   Ministry of Agriculture, Fisheries and Food, 1999, "MAFF BSE Information: Scheme Data". Available from www.maff.gov.uk/animalh/bse Accessed: 12/11/99.

32   UK Parliament, 1993, "Crop Residues (Burning) Regulations 1993". Statutory Instrument 1993 No.1355. HMSO: London. ISBN: 0110343662.

33   Hitchens D., Birnie E., McGowan A., Triebswetter U., Cottica A., 1998, "The Firm, Competitiveness and Environmental Regulations - A Study of the European Food Processing Industries". Edward Elgar: Cheltenham. ISBN: 9282739686.

34   Herzka A., Booth R.G., 1981, "Food Industry Wastes: Disposal and Recovery".
      Applied Science Publishers Ltd: England. ISBN: 0853349576.

35   Flores R.A., Shanklin C.W., 1998, "What's needed to use more agribusiness
      residues?" Biocycle, **39**(11), p82-83.

36   Birch G.G., Parker K.J., Worgan J.T., 1976, "Food from Waste". Applied
      Science Publishers Ltd: Essex. ISBN: 0853346593.

37   Moon N.J., Woodroof J.G., 1986, "Plant sanitation and waste disposal", p613-
      646. In: Commercial Fruit Processing, Woodroof J.G., Luh B.S (eds). AVI
      Publishing Co. Inc: Connecticut. ISBN: 0870555022.

38   Desphande M., Daniels L., 1995, "Evaluation of sophorolipid biosurfactant
      production by *Candida bombicola* using animal fat". Bioresource Technology,
      54(2), p143-150.

39   Larrauri J.A., Borroto B., Crespo A.R., 1997, "Water recycling in processing
      orange peel to a high dietary fibre powder". International Journal of Food
      Science and Technology, **32**(1), p73-76.

40   Coll M.D., Laencina J., Barberan F.A.T., 1998, "Recovery of flavanones from
      wastes of industrially processed lemons". Zeitschrift für Lebensmittel
      Untersuchung und Forschung A - Food Research and Technology, **206**(6),
      p404-407.

41   Mall I.D., 1995, "Waste utilisation and management in sugar and distillery
      plants". Chemical Engineering World, **30**(1), p51-60.

42   Israilides C.J., Smith A., Harthill J.E., Barnett C., Bambalov G., Scanlon B.,
      1998, "Pullulan content of the ethanol precipitate from fermented agro-
      industrial wastes". Applied Microbiology and Biotechnology, **49**(5), p613-617.

43   Gelinas P., McKinnon C.M., Pelletier M., 1999, "Sourdough-type bread from
      waste breadcrumb". Food Microbiology, **16**(1), p37-43.

44   Reeds J., 1998, "Realising waste elimination". Environment Business
      Magazine, No. 38, p27.

45   Benjakul S., Morrissey M.T., 1997, "Protein hydrolysates from Pacific Whiting solid wastes". Journal of Agriculture and Food Chemistry, **45**(9), p3423-3430.

46   Flair Flow Report, 1998, "Food Ingredients from Onion Waste", F-FE 307/98, as seen in Food Science and Technology Today, 1999, **13**(2), p75.

47   Olguin E.J., Doelle H.W., Mercado G., 1995, "Resource recovery through recycling of sugar processing by-products and residuals". Resource Conservation and Recycling, **15**(2), p85-94.

48   Borthakur P.C., Barkakati P., Bordoloi D., Sarkar S.L., 1993, "Producing black metal clinkers using rice husk as a fuel". World Cement, **24**(12), p45-49.

49   Anon, 1999, "Waste nut, want nut". New Scientist, No. 2213, p15.

50   Gathuo B., Rantala P., Maatta R., 1991, "Coffee industry wastes". Water Science and Technology, **24**(1), p53-60.

51   Abang Abdullah A.A., 1997, "Palm oil shell aggregate for lightweight concrete", p624-636. In: Waste Materials Used in Concrete Manufacturing, Chandra S. (ed). Noyes Publications: USA. ISBN: 0815513933.

52   Department of the Environment Transport and the Regions, 1998, "Digest of Environmental Statistics No. 20". The Stationery Office: London. ISBN: 0117534668. Also available from www.environment.detr.gov.uk/des20/index.htm

53   Tesco plc, 1996, "Annual Report and Accounts - 1996. Environment Information". Available from www.tesco.co.uk Accessed: 26/11/99.

54   Tesco plc, 1995, "Annual Report and Accounts - 1995. Investor Information". Available from www.tesco.co.uk Accessed: 26/11/99.

55   Anon, 1999, "Filtering out pollution". The Food & Grocery Industry in Action - A supplement to The Grocer, 11 Sept, p28.

56   US EPA Office of Solid Waste, 1998, "Don't throw that food away", EPA-530-F-98-023. Also available from www.epa.gov/osw

57   US EPA Office of Solid Waste, 1996, "Donating surplus food to the needy",
       EPA-530-F-96-038. Also available from www.epa.gov/osw

58   Tidy Britain Group, 1996 "Cleanliness Standards Survey of 58 UK Cities -
       1996". Tidy Britain Group. Summary available from www.tidybritain.org

59   Department of Environment, Transport and the Regions, 1999, "Code of
       Practice on Litter and Refuse". The Stationery Office: London. ISBN:
       011753479X.

60   Sydney Olympic Games Committee, 1999, "Green Games". Available from
       www.olympics.com/eng/about/green/recycling/home.html Accessed: 26/11/99.

61   Sydney Olympic Games Committee, 1999, "Integrated Waste Management
       Solution - The Strategy for the Sydney 2000 Games -". Available from
       www.olympics.com Accessed: 26/11/99.

62   SEPA, 1997, "Agriculture Leaflet: Agricultural Fuel Oil and Waste Oil".
       SEPA: Stirling. Also available from www.sepa.org.uk

63   SEPA, 1997, "Agriculture Leaflet: Silos and Silage Effluent". SEPA: Stirling.
       Also available from www.sepa.org.uk

64   Health and Safety Executive, 1997, "Sheep Dipping", Ref AS29 (rev2). HSE:
       Suffolk.

65   Ministry of Agriculture, Fisheries and Food, 1998, "Green Code - Code of
       Practice for the Safe Use of Pesticides on Farms and Holdings". PB3528.
       MAFF: London.

66   CCFRA, Horticulture Research International and Hortitech, 1999, "Integrated
       Crop Management: A system for fruit and vegetable crop production".
       Conference Proceedings held 25/2/99, CCFRA.

67   Knight C., 1998, "Pesticide controls in the food chain", Guideline No. 19.
       CCFRA: Gloucestershire. ISBN: 0905942124.

68   ETBPP, 1998, "Reducing the Cost of Cleaning in the Food and Drink
       Industry", GG154.

69   Ross C.C., Walsh J.L. and Valentine G.E., 1998, "Food processing wastes". Water Environment Research, **70**(4), p642-646.

70   ETBPP, 1996, "Cost-Effective Separation Technologies for Minimising Wastes and Effluents", GG37.

71   Environment Agency, SEPA, Environment & Heritage Service, 1998, "Schools and Educational Establishments". PPG16. Environment Agency: Reading. Also available from www.environment-agency.gov.uk or www.sepa.org.uk

72   Environment Agency, SEPA, Environment & Heritage Service, 1998, "Retail Stores". PPG15. Environment Agency: Reading. Also available from www.environment-agency.gov.uk or www.sepa.org.uk

73   US EPA Office of Air and Radiation, since 1995, "Food and Drink Industries", Chapter 9. In: AP42, 5th Edition, Volume 1. Available from www.epa.gov/ttnchie1/ap42c9.html Accessed: 25/11/99.

74   Department of the Environment, 1997, "Environmental Protection Act 1990 Part I. Secretary of State's Guidance - Vegetable Oil Extraction and Fat and Oil Refining Processes". PG6/25(97) 1997 Revision. The Stationery Office: London. ISBN: 0117533599.

75   Department of the Environment, 1997, "Environmental Protection Act 1990 Part I. Secretary of State's Guidance - Fish Meal and Fish Oil Processes". PG6/19(97) 1997 Revision. The Stationery Office: London. ISBN: 0117533580.

76   Department of the Environment, 1996, "Environmental Protection Act 1990 Part I. Secretary of State's Guidance - Vegetable Matter Drying Processes". PG6/27(96) 1996 Revision. The Stationery Office: London. ISBN: 0117533262.

77   Environmental Protection Agency, Ireland, 1996, "Integrated Pollution Control Licensing: BATNEEC Guidance Note for the Manufacture of Sugar", EPA LC18. EPA: Dublin. ISBN: 1899965386. Also available from www.epa.ie

78   Brunner C.R., 1989, "Handbook of Hazardous Waste Incineration". TAB Books Inc: USA. ISBN: 0830693181.

79 The Fresh Produce Consortium, 1999, "The Industry Guide to Good Hygiene Practice: Fresh Produce". Chadwick House Group: London. ISBN: 1902423194.

80 Royal Commission on Environmental Pollution, 1998, "12th Report: Best Practicable Environmental Option", Cm 310, as seen in DETR, "Waste Guide". Available from www.environment.detr.gov.uk/greening/waste/guide.htm Accessed: 8/11/99.

81 Anon, nd, "Environmental Glossary". Available from www.brad.ac.uk/acad/envsci/ET/glossary/enviglos.htm Accessed: 2/12/99.

82 Kirkpatric N., 1995, "Life Cycle Assessment". Available from www.wrfound.org.uk/previous/WB47-LCA.html Accessed: 5/11/99.

83 Williams P.T., 1998, "Waste Treatment and Disposal". Wiley: England. ISBN: 0471981494.

84 ETBPP, 1996, "Saving Money Through Waste Minimisation: Getting Started". Guide GS25.

85 ETBPP, 1999, "Reducing the Cost of Packaging in the Food and Drink Industry". Good Practice Guide GG157.

86 J Sainsbury plc, 1998, "J Sainsbury plc - 1998 Environment Report". J Sainsbury plc: London. Also available from www.j-sainsbury.co.uk/environment

87 Netwales, 1999, "Waste Exchange". Available from www.netwales.co.uk/WalesEn.Centre/wec/wastex.htm Accessed: November 1999.

88 Wastechange, 1999, "Waste Exchange". Available from www.wastechange.com/food.html Accessed: November 1999.

89 Anon, 1999, "Sainsbury's aims to kickstart 'Buy Recycled' campaign". Ends Report, No. 296, p34.

90   Institute of Wastes Management, 1994, "Down to earth composting of municipal green wastes" as seen in SEPA, 1998, "Strategic Review of Organic Waste Spread on Land". SEPA: Stirling. Also available from www.sepa.org.uk

91   James B., 1996, "An on-farm way of putting waste to use". Farmer's Weekly, 5 July, p85.

92   WRF, 1999, "Anaerobic Digestion". Available from www.wrf.org.uk/AD-15.html Accessed: 5/11/99.

93   The Compost Resource Page, nd, "Vermicomposting". Available from www.oldgrowth.org/compost/index.html Accessed: 8/11/99.

94   UK Parliament, 1991, "Control of Pollution (Silage, Slurry and Agricultural Fuel Oil) Regulations 1991". Statutory Instrument 1991 No. 324. HMSO: London. ISBN: 0110133242.

95   UK Parliament, 1989, "Sludge (Use in Agriculture) Regulations 1989". Statutory Instrument 1989 No. 1263. HMSO: London. ISBN: 0110972635.

96   Department of the Environment, 1992, "Code of Practice for the Agricultural Use of Sewage Sludge". HMSO: London. ISBN: 0117522562.

97   European Commission, 1986, "Council Directive of 12 June 1986 on the protection of the environment, and in particular of the soil, when sewage sludge is used in agriculture: 86/278/EEC". Official Journal, L181, p6-12.

98   Environment Agency, 1996, "Processes Subject to Integrated Pollution Control - Waste Incineration". IPC Guidance Note S2 5.01. The Stationery Office: London. ISBN: 0113101171.

99   Anon, 1997, "Reading FC set to kick off on transformed landfill site". Local Authority Waste & Environment, 5(12), p7, 16.

100 Dawson D., 2000, "Wastewater". Chapter in "Water quality for the food industry". CCFRA Guideline (in preparation)

101 SEPA, 1998, "Strategic Review of Organic Waste Spread on Land". SEPA: Stirling. Also available from www.sepa.org.uk

102 SEPA, 1997, "Agriculture Leaflet: Application of Non-Agricultural Waste to Land". SEPA: Stirling. Also available from www.sepa.org.uk

103 UK Parliament, 1998, "Fertilisers (Mammalian Meat and Bone Meal) Regulations 1998", Statutory Instrument 1998 No. 954. The Stationery Office: London. ISBN: 0110659120.

104 Anon, 1999, "Europe animal feed tainted with waste". Water and Waste International. Available from www.wwinternational.com/pages/updatecontent/Eufeed.html Accessed: 3/12/99.

105 Committee on the Microbiological Safety of Food, 1990, "The Microbiological Safety of Food". HMSO: London. Part I ISBN: 0113212739; Part II ISBN: 0113213476.

106 United Kingdom Agricultural Suppliers Trade Association, nd, "Overview - Feed". Available from www.ukasta.org.uk/about/overview/feed.htm Accessed: 3/12/99.

107 Crockett C., Sumar S., 1996, "The safe use of recycled and reused plastics in food contact materials - part I". Nutrition and Food Science, **3**, May/June, p32-37.

108 Castle L, 1994, "Recycled and re-used plastics for food packaging?". Packaging Technology and Science, **7**, p291-297.

109 EMAS, nd, "What is EMAS?". Available from www.emas.org.uk/what.htm Accessed: 10/11/99.

110 International Standards Organisation, nd, "ISO 14000". Available from www.iso.ch Accessed: 10/11/99.

111 Anon, 1998, "ISO 14001 certification tops 700 as EMAS trails behind", Ends Report, No. 286, p8.

112 Giese J.H., 1996, "ISO 14000 is coming". Food Technology, **50**(7), p34.

113 Stauffer J.E., 1997, "ISO 14000 Standards". Cereal Foods World, **42**(4), p228-230.

114 Boudouropoulos I.D., Arvanitoyannis I.S., 1998, "Current state and advances in the implementation of ISO 14000 by the food industry. Comparison of ISO14000 to ISO 9000 and other environmental programs". Trends in Food Science and Technology, **9**, p395-408.

115 Unilever, nd, "Foods". Available from www.unilever.com/public/env/review/environ/public/05food/05foodfr.htm Accessed: 10/11/99.

116 Andersson K., Ohlsson T., Olsson P., 1994, "Life cycle assessment (LCA) of food products and production systems". Trends in Food Science and Technology, **5**, p134-138.

117 Kusters J., 1999, "Life cycle approach to nutrient and energy efficiency in European Agriculture". Paper from The International Fertiliser Society, Proceeding No. 438, Cambridge 9/12/99. ISBN: 085310073X

118 Campden & Chorleywood Food Research Association Group, 1999, "Annual Review 1999". Campden & Chorleywood Food Research Association, Gloucestershire.

119 UK Parliament, 1998, "The Groundwater Regulations 1998", Statutory Instrument 1998 No. 2746. The Stationery Office: London. ISBN: 011079799X.

120 Royal Society of Chemistry, 1996, "Simple Guide on the Management and Control of Wastes". Royal Society of Chemistry: London. ISBN: 0854049908.

121 Croner Publications Ltd, since 1991, "Croner's Waste Management". Croner Publications Ltd: Surrey. ISBN: 185524117X.

122 Garner J.F., Harris D.J., Henderson H., Doolittle I.G. (eds), since 1976, "Garner's Environmental Law". Butterworths: UK. ISBN: 0406205108.

123 European Commission, 1996, "Council Directive 96/61/EC of 24 September 1996 concerning integrated pollution prevention and control." Official Journal, L257, 10/10/96, p26-40.

124 UK Parliament, 1999, "Pollution Prevention and Control Act 1999". HMSO: London. ISBN: 0105424994.

125 Anon, 1999, "Industry faces broader rules on pollution". Environment Action, Issue 22, October/November, p2.

126 UK Parliament, 1999, "Explanatory Notes to Pollution Prevention and Control Act 1999". HMSO: London. ISBN: 0105624993.

127 European Commission, 1994, "European Parliament and Council Directive 94/62/EC of 20 December 1994 on packaging and packaging waste". Official Journal, L365, 31/12/94, p1-23.

128 UK Parliament, 1997, "The Producer Responsibility Obligations (Packaging Waste) Regulations 1997", Statutory Instrument 1997 No. 648. The Stationery Office: London. ISBN: 011064106X

129 European Commission, 1991, "Council Directive 91/689/EEC of 12 December 1991 on hazardous waste." Official Journal, L377, 31/12/91, p20-27.

130 European Commission, 1994, "Council Decision of 22 December 1994 establishing a list of hazardous wastes pursuant to Article 1(4) of Council Directive 91/689/EEC." Official Journal, L356, 31/12/94, p14-22.

131 European Commission, 1999, "Council Directive 1999/31/EC of 26 April 1999 on the landfilling of waste." Official Journal, L182, 16/7/99, p1-19.

132 Department of Environment, Transport and the Regions, 1999, "Limiting Landfill: A Consultation Paper on Limiting Landfill to meet the EC Landfill Directive's Targets for the Landfill of Biodegradable Municipal Waste", 99EP0394. DETR: London. Also available at www.environment.detr.gov.uk

133 Department of Environment, Transport and the Regions, 1998, "Less Waste, More Value - Consultation Paper on the Waste Strategy for England and Wales". DETR: London. Available from www.environment.detr.gov.uk Accessed: November 1999.

134 UK Parliament, 1996, "Special Waste Regulations 1996", Statutory Instrument 1996 No. 972. HMSO: London. ISBN: 0110545656.

135 Department of the Environment, 1996, "Environmental Protection Act 1990: Special Waste Regulations 1996 Joint Circular", Circular 6/96. HMSO: London. ISBN: 01175332924.

136 Department of Environment, Transport and the Regions, 1999, "Changes ahead for packaging", Press Release No. 1139, 25/11/99. Available from www.detr.gov.uk Accessed: 25/11/99.

137 UK Parliament, 1996, "Landfill Tax Regulations", Statutory Instrument 1996, No. 1527. ISBN: 0110358929.

138 Entrust, nd, "Entrust - Achievement Brochure". Entrust: London. Available from www.entrust.org.uk Accessed: November 1999.

139 UK Parliament, 1999, "The Animal By-Products Order 1999", Statutory Instrument 1999 No. 646. The Stationery Office: London. ISBN: 0110822285.

140 UK Parliament, 1991, "The Water Resources Act 1991". HMSO: London. ISBN: 0105457914.

141 UK Parliament, 1991, "The Water Industry Act 1991". HMSO: London. ISBN: 0105456918.

142 UK Parliament, 1989, "Trade Effluent (Prescribed Processes and Substances) Regulations 1989", Statutory Instrument 1989 No. 1156. HMSO: London. ISBN: 0110971566.

143 UK Parliament, 1994, "The Urban Waste Water Treatment (England and Wales) Regulations 1994", Statutory Instrument 1994 No. 2841. HMSO: London. ISBN: 0110458419.

144 Information for Industry, nd, "Environmental Compliance Manual". Information for Industry Ltd: London. Chapter "Effluent and Water", various pages. Available from www.ifi.co.uk/ecm-eff.htm Accessed: 2/12/99.

145 Department of the Environment, 1996, "Environmental Protection Act 1990, Section 34: Waste Management Duty of Care - A Code of Practice". HMSO: London. ISBN: 0111753210X.

146 Environment Agency, SEPA, 1997, "Pollution Prevention Guidelines: The Prevention of Pollution of Controlled Waters by Pesticides", PPG9. Environment Agency: Bristol. Also available from www.environment-agency.gov.uk and www.sepa.org.uk

147 Environment Agency, SEPA, 1997, "Pollution Prevention Guidelines: Dairies and Other Milk Handling Operations", PPG17. Environment Agency: Bristol. Also available from www.environment-agency.gov.uk and www.sepa.org.uk

148 Environment Agency, 1998, "Combustion of Meat and Bone Meal", Amplification Note 1 S2 1.05. Available from www.environment-agency.gov.uk Accessed: November 1999.

149 Environment Agency, 1998, "Animal Remains Incineration", Amplification Note 1 S2 1.05. Available from www.environment-agency.gov.uk Accessed: November 1999.

150 European Integrated Pollution Control Bureau, nd. Available from eippcb.jrc.es Accessed: 5/11/99.

151 Gurnham, C.F., 1965, "Industrial Wastewater Control". Academic Press: London.

152 Macrory R., 1998, "High court rules on recycling", Ends Report, No. 286, November, p46-47.

153 British Agrochemicals Association, 1998, "Container Incineration - A Practical Guide". British Agrochemicals Centre, Peterborough.

154 BRC, WaterUK, ADAS, 1999, "The Safe Sludge Matrix - Guidelines for the Application of Sewage Sludge to Agricultural Land". ADAS Gleadthorpe Research Centre.

155 European Commission, 1991, "Council Directive 91/156/EEC of 18 March 1991 amending Directive 75/442/EEC on waste". Official Journal, L78, 26/3/1991, p. 32-27.

156 UK Parliament, 1994, "The Waste Management Licensing Regulations, 1994". Statutory Instrument 1994, No. 1056. HMSO: London. ISBN: 0110440560

157 UK Parliament, 1994, "Environmental Protection Act 1990: Part II. Waste Management Licensing. The Framework Directive on Waste". DoE Circular 11/94. HMSO: London. ISBN: 0117529753.

158 UK Parliament, 1991, "The Controlled Waste (Registration of Carriers and Seizure of Vehicles) Regulations 1991. Statutory Instrument 1991 No. 1624. HMSO: London. ISBN: 0110146247.

159 Environment Agency, SEPA, Environment and Heritage Service, DETR, HSE, 1999, "Special Wastes: a technical guidance note on their definition and classification. Volume I: Legislation framework and assessment methodology". The Stationery Office: London. ISBN: 0113101589.

ABBREVIATIONS AND ACRONYMS

BAT	Best Available Technology
BATNEEC	Best Available Technology Not Entailing Excessive Cost
BOD	Biological Oxygen Demand
BPEO	Best Practicable Environmental Option
BSE	Bovine Spongiform Encephalopathy
CADDET	Centre for Analysis and Dissemination of Demonstrated Energy Technologies
CHP	Combined Heat and Power
COD	Chemical Oxygen Demand
DETR	Department of Environment, Transport and the Regions
EC	European Commission
EU	European Union
HMIP	Her Majesty's Inspectorate of Pollution
IPC	Integrated Pollution Control
IPPC	Integrated Pollution Prevention and Control
LARAC	Local Authority Recycling Advisory Committee

MAFF	Ministry of Agriculture, Fisheries and Food
nd	no date
PCBs	Polychlorinated Biphenyls
PCTs	Polychlorinated Terphenyls
PM	Particulate Matter
SEPA	Scottish Environment Protection Agency
SOAEFD	Scottish Office for Agriculture, Environment and Fisheries Department
VOCs	Volatile Organic Compounds
WTE	Waste to Energy

ABOUT CCFRA

The Campden & Chorleywood Food Research Association (CCFRA) is the largest membership-based food and drink research centre in the world. It provides wide-ranging scientific, technical and information services to companies right across the food production chain - from growers and producers, through processors and manufacturers to retailers and caterers. In addition to its 1500 members (drawn from over 50 different countries), CCFRA serves non-member companies, industrial consortia, UK government departments, levy boards and the European Union.

The services provided range from field trials of crop varieties and evaluation of raw materials through product and process development to consumer and market research. There is significant emphasis on food safety (e.g. through HACCP), hygiene and prevention of contamination, food analysis (chemical, microbiological and sensory), factory and laboratory auditing, training and information provision. As part of the latter, CCFRA publishes a wide range of research reports, good manufacturing practice guides, reviews, videos, databases, software packages and alerting bulletins. These activities are under-pinned by fully-equipped modern food processing halls, product development facilities, extensive laboratories, a purpose-built training centre and a centralised information service.

In 1998 CCFRA established a wholly owned subsidiary in Hungary from where an experienced team of scientists and technologists provides training and consultancy on HACCP, quality management, product development, market and consumer research, food and environment law, and hygiene to Eastern Europe.

To find out more, visit the CCFRA website at www.campden.co.uk